Chris Hodges's book *Fresh Air* explains how to experience a freshness in your life and relationship with God that you may not have realized was possible. Instead of a list of Christian how-to's or quick fixes, it takes readers inward, leading them on a spiritual journey of transformation from the inside out. Chris's personal experiences and humorous anecdotes make this book an engaging read. I recommend it!

JOHN C. MAXWELL
Leadership expert, author, and speaker

Inspiring and practical, *Fresh Air* is a must-read for anyone who wants more out of life. Best of all, the insightful and power-filled principles in this book are ones that anyone can apply.

MARK BATTERSON
Lead pastor, National Community Church, Washington, DC;
New York Times bestselling author

Chris Hodges is being used by God in our generation to bring new insights and leadership to the church. Discover the powerful secrets of a God-breathed life and enjoy the fresh air of God's blessing.

STEVEN FURTICK
Lead pastor, Elevation Church; author of Sun Stand Still

If anyone can honestly tell you what it means to live a vibrant life with God, Chris can. He is one of America's best teachers of God's Word. There is a critical need for the message in this book because many Christians have grown cold and stale. No matter where you are in your walk with God, you can use some fresh air. Pick up this book and get ready to breathe again.

RICK BEZET
Lead pastor, New Life Church of Arkansas

We all know what it is like to feel stuck, when it seems like we are going nowhere fast. In times like that, the breath of God makes all the difference. It renews us; it changes hearts and attitudes. *Fresh Air* reminds us that if we seek God, he will never fail to change us from the inside out.

GREG SURRATT
Lead pastor, Seacoast Church; author of Ir-Rev-Rend

Too many people feel stuck in life. It's a common problem with a solution few consider: the Holy Spirit. In *Fresh Air*, Chris shows how to live a life empowered by the Spirit—and he does it without ever being weird! I am so encouraged whenever I spend time with Chris. As you read this book, I know you'll feel the same way.

ROBERT MORRIS
Senior pastor, Gateway Church; bestselling author of The Blessed Life, From Dream to Destiny, *and* The God I Never Knew

The heart of the Father resonates throughout the pages of *Fresh Air*, and the insights will become divine and meaningful treasures in your heart. Your own witness will then become a breath of fresh life to others.

JAMES ROBISON
Founder and president, LIFE Outreach International

So often we find ourselves in what Chris refers to as the doldrums—a spiritual state where we feel lifeless, bored, and without hope amidst the routines of life. We know there is more, and long for it, but we aren't quite sure how to get there. Whether it's finding passion in your marriage again, discovering true fulfillment in your career, or actually enjoying time in the spiritual disciplines, *Fresh Air* unpacks what it looks like to have a new life full of vision, purpose, passion, and hope.

CHRISTINE CAINE
Founder, The A21 Campaign

I love this book! *Fresh Air* will help you escape the mundane treadmill of living by empty rules and striving for empty success. With authenticity and clarity, Chris points us to the person who makes life fun again: Jesus.

JUDAH SMITH
Lead pastor, The City Church

Fresh Air is an uplifting book that will bring a renewed sense of purpose into your life. Chris Hodges shows why peace and fulfillment come from a strong connection to Jesus Christ on the inside. He will teach you how to breathe new life into your attitudes, your relationships, your finances, and the way you see yourself.

MATTHEW BARNETT
Cofounder, The Dream Center; senior pastor, Angelus Temple; author, The Cause within You

Chris's heart to see individuals flourish in their spiritual journey is a "breath of fresh air," and I believe that as you read this book, you will receive life-giving words of encouragement and an awakened sense of calling and purpose. Allow the Holy Spirit to refresh and inspire you as you begin to understand what it means to live a God-breathed life.

BRIAN HOUSTON
Senior pastor, Hillsong Church

With amazing candidness, Pastor Chris unveils the secret of an inner life that is full, thrilling, and invigorating. He balances the Spirit-led life with the divine order of the Spirit to produce a life-giving lifestyle. I have known Chris for more than thirty years and know of no more humble, yielded, pure vessel. He truly is a breath of fresh air.

LARRY STOCKSTILL
Pastor, Bethany World Prayer Center

This book will change your thinking and help you to revive every area of your life. Chris's authenticity and transparency are vital to this generation of Christ-followers. Live the life God intended for you—don't settle for anything less!

DINO RIZZO
Lead pastor, Healing Place Church; author, Servolution

A brilliant must-read! If you've ever experienced staleness in your life or simply desire a richer, fuller life in God, you will be encouraged by the message in these pages. *Fresh Air* will bring newness to your walk with God and revival to your soul.

STOVALL WEEMS
Lead pastor, Celebration Church

FRESH AIR

*trading stale spiritual obligation for a life-altering,
energizing, experience-it-everyday relationship with God*

CHRIS HODGES

TYNDALE
MOMENTUM

An Imprint of
Tyndale House Publishers, Inc.

Visit Tyndale online at www.tyndale.com. Visit Tyndale Momentum online at www.tyndale momentum.com. *TYNDALE* is a registered trademark of Tyndale House Publishers, Inc. *Tyndale Momentum* and the Tyndale Momentum logo are trademarks of Tyndale House Publishers, Inc. Tyndale Momentum is an imprint of Tyndale House Publishers, Inc.

Fresh Air: Trading Stale Spiritual Obligation for a Life-Altering, Energizing, Experience-It-Everyday Relationship with God

Designed by Barry Smith and Dean H. Renninger

Published in association with the literary agency of Winters and King, Inc., 2448 E. 81st St., CityPlex Towers, Suite 5900, Tulsa, OK 74137.

All Scripture quotations, unless otherwise indicated, are taken from the Holy Bible, *New International Version,*® *NIV.*® Copyright © 1973, 1978, 1984, 2011 by Biblica, Inc.™ (Some quotations used are from the 1984 edition of the *NIV.*) Used by permission of Zondervan. All rights reserved worldwide. www.zondervan.com.

Scripture quotations marked NLT are taken from the *Holy Bible*, New Living Translation, copyright © 1996, 2004, 2007 by Tyndale House Foundation. Used by permission of Tyndale House Publishers, Inc., Carol Stream, Illinois 60188. All rights reserved.

Scripture quotations marked TLB are taken from *The Living Bible*, copyright © 1971 by Tyndale House Foundation. Used by permission of Tyndale House Publishers, Inc., Carol Stream, Illinois 60188. All rights reserved.

Scripture quotations marked KJV are taken from the *Holy Bible*, King James Version.

Scripture quotations marked AMP are taken from the *Amplified Bible,*® copyright © 1954, 1958, 1962, 1964, 1965, 1987 by The Lockman Foundation. Used by permission.

Scripture quotations marked *The Message* are taken from *The Message* by Eugene H. Peterson, copyright © 1993, 1994, 1995, 1996, 2000, 2001, 2002. Used by permission of NavPress Publishing Group. All rights reserved.

Scripture quotations marked ESV are taken from *The Holy Bible*, English Standard Version® (ESV®), copyright © 2001 by Crossway, a publishing ministry of Good News Publishers. Used by permission. All rights reserved.

Scripture quotations marked NASB are taken from the New American Standard Bible,® copyright © 1960, 1962, 1963, 1968, 1971, 1972, 1973, 1975, 1977, 1995 by The Lockman Foundation. Used by permission.

Scripture quotations marked NKJV are taken from the New King James Version.® Copyright © 1982 by Thomas Nelson, Inc. Used by permission. All rights reserved. *NKJV* is a trademark of Thomas Nelson, Inc.

Scripture quotations marked NCV are taken from the New Century Version.® Copyright © 2005 by Thomas Nelson, Inc. Used by permission. All rights reserved. *NCV* is a trademark of Thomas Nelson, Inc.

Library of Congress Cataloging-in-Publication Data

Hodges, Chris.
   Fresh air : Trading Stale Spiritual Obligation for a Life-Altering, Energizing, Experience-It-Everyday Relationship with God / Chris Hodges.
      p. cm.
   Includes bibliographical references.
   ISBN 978-1-4143-7125-2
1. Christian life. 2. Holy Spirit. I. Title.
   BV4501.3.H625 2012
   248.4 —dc23   2012020883

Printed in the United States of America

18	17	16	15	14	13	12
7	6	5	4	3	2	1

To the amazing people of Church of the Highlands:
So much of this book came from what we experienced together.
You are a breath of fresh air to me.

CONTENTS

PART 3 FINDING THE SOURCE OF BREATH

FOREWORD

Have you ever met someone who had something you didn't have?

I'm not talking about a person who had a cool fishing boat, a cute boyfriend, or a full-size bowling alley in the basement. I'm referring to something different, something internal. He or she had some inner quality that was difficult to describe but impossible to miss. It might have been an unmistakable joy, an unshakable faith, an undeniable peace, or something else you wanted—but didn't have.

Chris Hodges was a person like that for me.

In the summer of 2006 I was slowly sinking under the weight of way too many commitments. When a friend asked me for a personal favor, my mind raced with excuses. Instinctively, I blurted out something about how busy I was, the only reasonable defense I could come up with in the moment.

My friend didn't take no for an answer. "I really believe you should meet this guy. He's a pastor, like you. I can't tell you why, but I'm just asking you this one time, will you meet with him for me?"

I reluctantly agreed to a one-hour meeting with Chris Hodges. Little did I know that our brief meeting would extend into a three-day weekend and grow into one of the closest friendships I've ever known.

There was something about Chris that grabbed my attention and wouldn't let go. Like me, he was leading a growing church. (In fact, I don't know if I've seen a church in the United States grow faster than his.) For me, the weight of leading our church seemed more like a burden than a blessing. Chris, on the other hand, seemed to walk lighter, rest better, and enjoy life at a deeper level than I did. At first I dismissed it as a difference in personality types, but then I discovered that he's a type A personality like me. The more time we spent together, the more I had to admit that our differences weren't practical or physical. They were unquestionably spiritual.

Chris seemed to live with more of God's presence.

On a trip to his church, Church of the Highlands in Birmingham, Alabama, I finally asked Chris point-blank, "What's different about you?"

And that's when Chris started to tell me his story, the same one he'll share with you in this book. For starters, he hadn't always been as intimate with God. In fact, he'd been consistently overwhelmed, hurting, and deeply depressed. Chris explained in detail how he learned to do life and ministry empowered by the Holy Spirit. His thoughts weren't spooky or odd; they were very biblical and surprisingly practical.

With his encouragement, I sought God during my first twenty-one-day fast (something Chris had done with his church for years). Seeking the heart of God while denying my body physical nutrition unleashed something special inside of me. God's Word, God's people, and God's presence became a bigger part of my life—more so than ever before. God started to change me, heal me, cleanse me.

The people closest to me noticed the changes too. Now I'm not just serving God. I'm loving God, enjoying God, knowing God. And the difference is bigger than I could ever adequately explain.

That's why I'm so thankful that you're holding this book. I believe God wants to use Chris's life, his story, and his wisdom to help you fall more in love with God than you ever have before. As you read, I can assure you that Chris lives what he teaches. And he will help you exchange an increasingly stress-filled life for a God-honoring, world-changing, Spirit-filled life.

It's time for a breath of fresh air.

Craig Groeschel

PART 1

SEARCHING FOR A BREATH OF FRESH AIR

CHAPTER 1

THE DOLDRUMS

....

We were almost lost in the middle of the Pacific.
We almost capsized in those doldrums.
ROBERT ANDERSON

Most mornings I wake up happy and optimistic, looking forward to another day. I've never been a depressed kind of guy. But in 1999 I had the worst year of my life. On paper everything looked perfect, and there were no external clues pointing to my interior struggle. My wife loved me and our children were healthy. The church where I was an associate pastor was a thriving, growing community of passionate believers. I had even been doing some consulting for other churches that were interested in using our church as a model for their growth plans. There was money in the bank and the bills were paid. I had friends, both old ones I'd known since high school and new ones in our neighborhood, who genuinely liked me and seemed to care about me.

But I had never felt more miserable.

Despite all the good things in my life, I had been experiencing some new challenges: difficult relationships that grew more complicated because of miscommunication and distrust, worries about the future and meeting the financial needs of our expanding family, a stale spiritual life with little desire to spend time in prayer or Scripture, uncertainty about whether I was where God wanted me to be. Was I really cut out to be a pastor? Somehow I just couldn't envision myself doing the same thing for the rest of my life, but when I thought about it, I wasn't sure what I envisioned for the rest of my life.

In the deepest part of me I wondered, *Is this all there is?*

As the weeks dragged on, I became mired in a swamp of unpleasant emotions that I wasn't used to feeling—at least not all at once and not with such increasing intensity. I was deeply sad, but I wasn't sure why. I sensed anger and frustration, but that was probably because I felt so stuck in my sadness. And then there was the fear. I had never experienced anything like this and didn't know what to make of it.

So I hid it as long as I could and tried to pretend there wasn't a storm cloud constantly roiling around inside me. It seemed to grow darker, with more thunder rumblings and lightning strikes of acute emotion, yet the storm never broke and continued to gather itself over and over again inside my mind and heart.

I knew I was depressed but hated to admit that even to myself. I had never been depressed before and had even been quietly critical of those who seemed to fight an ongoing battle with it. I had always thought, *Just choose to be happy and get on with your life, buddy!* But now those thoughts mocked me because I wasn't sure how to change what I felt inside. I couldn't pinpoint exactly what my feelings were, but I knew I couldn't change them simply by telling myself, *Don't worry, be happy.*

Similarly, I didn't know how to fix the problem. I wasn't sure if it was spiritual or physical, mental or emotional, or all the above. So I did what so many of us do: I forced myself to go through the motions. At church staff meetings, I acted like I couldn't be happier, nodding and smiling, detached from the storm inside me. I'd go home and try to act normal, dismissing any signs of discouragement my wife, Tammy, or our kids noticed with, "I'm okay—just tired."

This went on for months. Then in January of 2000, our church focused on a prayer effort called "21 Days of Prayer," a time of personal fasting, prayer, and listening for God in our lives. Everyone was asked to participate at whatever level they felt led. This was the fourth time our church had started the year this way, and I had always been involved, although not very seriously.

But this time I was so desperate to hear from God that I went to extremes. Figuring the new year might be my opportunity for a fresh start, I went on a complete fast: no food, no media, no distractions. I would only pray and read my Bible. I was determined to give this a shot and had committed to going to the doctor afterward if this time alone with God didn't reveal what was going on. (I probably should have gone for a checkup already, but my stubborn ego kept thinking I could handle it.)

And then on day 17 of my fast, God visited me during one of the morning prayer services at our church as I was worshiping and seeking him in prayer. I'll never forget that moment, and it remains one of the seminal events of my entire life. His presence was so real, his voice so clear, that the storm inside me broke. Like the sensation of a cool, refreshing rain falling after the heat and humidity of a summer thunderstorm, his presence revived me. I also received a picture in my heart, an image of me leading a congregation of people. Up until that point, I had never even considered being a senior or lead pastor. In my seventeen years of ministry, I had never wanted anything more than to be the best number two guy on the planet. God spoke to my heart and said that he would lead me to something that year and it would be my assignment for the rest of my life.

TURNING POINT

Now this may not sound like much, but it gave me tremendous hope. Shortly after the fast was over, I met with my pastor, Larry Stockstill, and learned that God had spoken to him, too. It was time for me to launch out and lead a church of my own, Larry said, and he wanted to help me. From then on, one door opened after another, and God made it clear what path he wanted me to follow. I quickly became more passionate, more excited, and more alive than I'd ever been before. And I know I would never have gotten there if not for experiencing that year in the doldrums.

God used that time of desperation and depression to get my attention in the most dramatic way possible. Apparently, it often takes something painful, sometimes even tragic, to get us to listen to God. But that time of prayer and fasting was like a breath of fresh air. The fast disconnected me from the world, and my prayer time connected me to God. Looking back, I suspect God was talking all along and I just couldn't hear him. Somehow I had sensed this and become very sad that I was missing out on the huge heart message he wanted to give me. My depression forced me to stop and listen.

Today, I pastor one of the fastest growing congregations in the country, a dynamic, life-giving church that I love. I've often thought that I wouldn't even be a pastor here in Birmingham, Alabama, if I had not gone through that difficult time of feeling stuck. I had to find a way to move through it and allow God's breath to fill my sails.

Maybe you struggle with depression or have gone through a season like the one I described. You might even feel like you're going through the motions right now, unsure what's wrong but definitely sure that something's not right. Perhaps the hardest part is that your faith feels thin and flimsy, unable to bear whatever it is that's rumbling deep inside you.

Maybe you grew up in the church and know all the right things to say and do. Or maybe religion was not a part of your upbringing—you or your parents didn't see any real joy in the lives of those people who claimed to be filled with the love of Jesus. Or maybe you've experienced this kind of going-through-the-motions numbness in other areas of your life. At work. In your marriage. With your kids. In your friendships. You're waiting for something to happen, for the storm inside you to break, for a fresh breeze to breathe new life into you. You're not sure how to make it happen. But you know there has to be more.

THERE HAS TO BE MORE

There's something amazing about feeling a warm ocean breeze across your face from the deck of a ship. And watching the wind fill a giant piece of canvas, tilting that large sail in a way that both powers and directs the vessel, is even more incredible. Before the age of motorized boats, merchants, explorers, and sailors relied on these trade winds to carry them to certain places, especially across the ocean to another country or continent. You've probably seen enough *Pirates of the Caribbean* movies to know this, if you haven't been out on a sailboat yourself.

You may be waiting for a fresh breeze to breathe new life into you. You're not sure how to make it happen, but you know there has to be more.

Prior to the twentieth century, however, all mariners knew about one area that was to be avoided at all costs: the Doldrums. Taken from the root word meaning "dull" or "lifeless," the expression "in the doldrums" was used to describe the state of being bored and restless, in a slump. Sailors then gave this name to a specific region along the equator where the weather always seemed to illustrate this lifeless condition.

Because of the way the earth rotates, the currents and clouds of the Northern Hemisphere literally collide with the winds and weather of the Southern Hemisphere, creating an area of unpredictable weather. Usually extending between five degrees latitude north and five degrees latitude south of the equator, the Doldrums are also known as the Intertropical Convergence Zone (ITCZ).

Normal trade winds converge in this band along the equator and basically cancel each other out, creating a still, windless dead zone. Their collision also produces convectional storms that result in some of the world's heaviest precipitation. Since there's no wind to move them along, just an air mass hovering overhead, these storms keep sailing ships stuck in place.

It's not surprising, then, that the Doldrums were once feared more than the Bermuda Triangle. Many ships became trapped in the dead zone, forced to endure grueling storms until they wrecked. Sailors would try everything they knew to do to get the ship sailing again, but nothing worked. They were stuck, sometimes permanently.

While our GPS systems and hydraulic engine technology now protect ships from the dangers of the equatorial Doldrums, its emotional equivalent seems more prevalent than ever. We still use this figure of speech to describe someone who's in a slump, listless, despondent, stagnant, and going through the motions. I can't think of a better word to describe what I experienced in my church growing up, and then later as a young adult when I found myself back in a spiritual performance trap.

I think most of us can relate to being in the doldrums. You may know what you're supposed to do in life, you may even know where you want to go, but you are stuck in this zone where there's no wind, no breath, no life, nothing to help motivate you and move you along. Maybe you're going through a storm and doing all you can just to stay afloat. Maybe it's been a long time since you've been fired up about anything. Maybe you're in a rut and don't know how to move forward.

There's usually no single reason for you to feel immobilized like this. Like cool air colliding with tropical winds over the ocean, your doldrums may be the result of a number of factors converging. Nonetheless, it's usually helpful to think about what has contributed to your present location in life. Let's quickly look at some reasons you may find yourself stuck in the doldrums.

DRIFT AWAY

Have you ever spent a lazy day at the beach, riding the waves and bodysurfing? I love doing this with our kids, but it's always amazing where we find ourselves after we've been out in the water for an hour or two. We look back at the shore and suddenly nothing looks familiar. We can't see our umbrella or beach chairs—sometimes we can't even see our hotel! Without realizing it, we have drifted with the current and lost our bearings.

Without a strong direction toward a place where God is moving, without a secure anchor to keep you grounded, it's easy to drift into a dead zone. You may be doing all the right things—at home, at work, at church—but you don't know where your life is headed. You feel lost and disoriented from where you thought you'd be and how you thought you'd get there. But it's almost too terrifying to acknowledge, so you just keep going with the flow day after day.

When I was reading about the Doldrums that sailors face, I was struck by the fact that this dangerous dead zone happens along the equator. When ships got trapped there, it meant they weren't really in the Northern Hemisphere or the Southern Hemisphere; they were stuck where the two meet. I think we often get stuck in a similar manner. If we're honest, we know we don't want to go to hell, but yet we don't really want to serve God, either. We want to have one foot in the world and the other in the Kingdom of God. We want to straddle the spiritual equator, so to speak.

A lot of us have drifted to this place. We're not on fire for God, but of course we're not living for the devil either. We're not abandoning God and leaving the church, but we're not fully alive and enjoying the abundant life Jesus said he came to bring. We're in this middle zone, a spiritual no-man's-land.

A lot of us have drifted to a spiritual no-man's-land.

We have gotten off course, and now there's no wind to sustain us. This isn't a new phenomenon. Jesus tells the church at Laodicea,

"Some of you are not hot [not in the Northern Hemisphere], you are not even cold [not in the Southern Hemisphere], you are lukewarm." And the result is just as disastrous: "There is no life there. I will spit you out of my mouth [if I find you in that lukewarm zone]" (see Revelation 3:15-16).

In his letter to the church at Corinth, Paul conveyed a similar message: he told them that he could not consider them spiritual, but he could not call them worldly either. They were a mixture of the two. They were carnal (see 1 Corinthians 3:1, KJV). The word *carnal* means that they were stuck in the flesh. The word's root comes through in a usage you may be more familiar with: chili con carne—chili with meat. Paul basically said these Corinthian Christians were serving up a big dish of faith con carne. They were Christians but still had some flesh-based living in them.

Many of us today follow the same recipe. We want enough Jesus to get us to heaven, but we've got a little bit of the world in us too. We're lukewarm, tepid, not hot or cold, not heavenly and not earthly, not sold out to God and not entirely through renting from the devil. So we drift away and get stuck in the doldrums.

EYE OF THE STORM

Sometimes we don't drift into the spiritual doldrums but are pushed there by life's disturbances. In fact, the doldrums are a magnet for life's storms. The storms will either get us there and keep us there, or else they will happen while we're there. A huge part of the problem is that most of us don't respond to storms correctly. Instead of running to God for shelter and protection, we run from him, usually right into the eye of the storm.

When the storm winds are blowing and life gets hard, many people feel like they've done something wrong—perhaps even something to deserve their present crisis—and therefore they stay away from God. After all, he'll only punish them more, right? Or when times get hard, they seem to think that God hasn't kept his end of the bargain. They went to church, prayed, read their Bibles, served those around them—and now this is how God repays them? They feel like they did everything they were supposed to do and had the right to expect God to prevent trials from happening in their lives.

So we get stuck in the doldrums and may even come to view ourselves as victims. No matter what happens, we always seem to be heading into another storm. Maybe it's losing our job or watching our retirement fund shrink to less than where it started. Maybe it's an ongoing illness or injury, if not our own then that of our kids or someone else we love. It could be that our marriage has lost its passion and now we feel stuck in a lifeless relationship. How are we supposed to cope with any one of these crises, let alone the perfect storm that occurs when they collide?

For some people, the answer becomes a secret addiction, a way of numbing the pain by finding a few fleeting moments of pleasure. It could be alcohol or prescription drugs, shopping and then shopping some more, watching porn and withdrawing from our spouses, chatting with a sympathetic stranger online, or staying busy with work 24-7.

We try anything to keep ourselves from thinking about the storms in which we find ourselves—anything to ease the pain. And yet these attempts to gain relief only create more storms as we come to rely on our addictions. Once again, we discover that we are unable to move.

LOSING OUR BALANCE

So often doldrums are the result of weariness and spiritual fatigue. Like a sailor with no compass and no sense of direction, we find ourselves aimlessly following others' wishes, having lost the ability to say no. We don't want to disappoint anyone, right? So we try to do it all—to be the supermom or the perfect dad; to climb the corporate ladder; to lead the Bible study; to head up the kids' fund-raising drive; to stay on top of the household chores.

The result? We burn out and become cynical, angry, frustrated, and soul weary. Our marriages, which started out so beautifully, now seem more like an arrangement of convenience in which two roommates share possessions and custody of the kids. We secretly resent and withdraw from each other. The job that energized our careers and brought us such excitement now comes at us like a double-decker bus, one that we seem to get thrown under by everyone at the office.

The people who were once our friends now really annoy us because it seems like they always want something from us. They call and rant on and on about their problems, never once asking how we are doing. The kids seem only to need more and more while saying thank you less and less. More chauffeuring, more money, more help with homework. And if it's not the kids needing us, it's our own parents, becoming more and more reliant on our help as they age.

We feel like there's no one to talk to, no one who understands all the responsibility we carry. We're so unbearably lonely, even when there are dozens of people around. We bury our emotions just below the surface because we're afraid that if we release them, they will overwhelm us and we'll never function again. We've lost our sense of balance and now neglect the basics. In fact, we've lost not only a sense of balance in our lives but a sense of purpose. The joy of knowing who we are and what God created us to do seems like a distant memory at best.

We're burned out, weary to the bone, scared, and anxious—and there's no end in sight. The doldrums spin us 'round and 'round, and we don't know which way is up. God sure doesn't seem to care enough to do anything about where we are. So we carry our pain alone and try to keep going for one more day.

JUST BE IT

A friend once told me about an experience he had when he was in college. He and some buddies were enjoying one of the first warm days of spring by going swimming in the mountain streams nearby. Their destination was a place called "the sink," which featured a beautiful, dramatic, twenty-foot waterfall with a perfect lagoon below for swimming. There was even a cliff on the opposite side with a ledge that was ideal for jumping or diving.

So after horsing around for a while, my friend told me he jumped from the ledge into the water below. Only when he tried to come up, he found himself directly beneath the pounding stream of the waterfall. He began swimming harder, but the undertow of the waterfall pulled him right back beneath it. Starting to panic and running out of air, my friend began paddling frantically toward the shallow end of the lagoon. He could hear his friends talking and laughing— they hadn't noticed his predicament yet—but he couldn't break the surface.

Finally, after several minutes, my friend said he realized that he was going to die. He had exhausted himself in the struggle to swim free of the vortex of water created by the falls above. So he stopped paddling and allowed the water to push him deeper still. But after sinking several feet, his body suddenly shot like a torpedo to the surface and through the falls!

Gasping for air, he realized that only when he had completely surrendered did the undercurrent release him from its grasp. If he had relaxed and floated sooner, he wouldn't have exhausted himself and risked drowning. He had to quit working so hard to save himself if he wanted to live.

The doldrums often affect us in a similar way. We find ourselves in a storm or just in a rut, and suddenly we think we'd better try harder. If only we'd exercise more, stay later at the office, help out with the household chores more, spend more quality time with the kids, pray more often, read the Bible every day . . . well, then everything would be all right. But, of course, we only end up burned out and on the brink of spiritual, physical, and emotional exhaustion.

The doldrums flourish when we're focused on doing rather than being. We forget that real life happens internally more than externally. We would rather *do* something than *be* something.

There are always two ways to determine behavior—the internal motivation and the external motivation. In other words, every behavior is motivated either by an internal force or an external force. I can drive at a safe speed out of concern for my safety and the safety of the people around me or I can do it because of the sign on the highway that tells me I have to drive at a certain speed. I can be faithful to my wife out of my love for her or I can attempt to be faithful in obedience to the law that says, "Thou shalt not commit adultery." I believe there's a constant tension in us and in our society between internal motivation and the use of external constraints to determine our behavior.

> *The doldrums flourish when we're focused on doing rather than being.*

It's always much easier to have an external rule to make us behave. But while rules are important, that's not the gospel. The Good News that Jesus brought is about a transformation of the inner person that makes us different at our core.

If you're ever going to make it out of the doldrums and stay out, then it comes back to your inner motivation. Why do you do what you do? What do you want to do with your life? Where do you want to go?

The purpose of this book is to put wind in your sails again. To get you unstuck. To move you through the storm. To help you reclaim your compass and redirect your course. Heaven knows, we don't need another motivational, inspirational, feel-good self-help book. I'm not saying that these books aren't helpful or even biblically based— just that there are plenty of them. Most of them focus on changing behaviors and cultivating habits. Again, that's not necessarily bad; it's just inadequate for making lasting change.

You can focus on externals all you want and try to imitate the methods of others in hopes of duplicating their success, purpose, or happiness. But you'll only end up on the treadmill of disappointment, more frustrated than before, unless you make changes on the inside first.

If you want a breath of fresh air in your life that will resuscitate your spirit and bring you closer to God—and closer to being the person he made you to be—then this book is for you. I'm convinced that if you pursue God, you'll experience a passion and a zeal for living while enjoying every dimension of your life like never before. You will discover the X factor—that rare, life-giving quality that we will explore further in the next chapter—and it will manifest itself in everything you do.

In part 2, we'll look at some of the practices that helped me follow after God and escape the doldrums. Although these practices are not in themselves the secret to a changed life, I believe they are a means to access the power that can change yours.

Yes, it will require some changes, some discipline, and some perseverance. But if you stick with it, then you'll never have to worry about remaining stuck in the doldrums again.

BREATHING LESSON

Perhaps you haven't sensed a fresh breath in your life for a long time. You may have gotten out of touch with the way God is active and moving in your world. If so, you may have difficulty even pinpointing the cause or determining the route back into the open air.

If you find yourself in the doldrums today, my hope is that this book will refresh you. My twenty-one-day fast was a catalyst to get me going again, and I want to encourage you to invite God to come alongside you and begin to revitalize you with his healing wind as well. And be encouraged: as painful as the doldrums are, God will use this stuck place to do a great work in you. Be assured, when something is happening to you, God wants to do something in you.

> We were crushed and overwhelmed beyond our
> ability to endure, and we thought we would never live
> through it. In fact, we expected to die. But as a result,
> we stopped relying on ourselves and learned to rely
> only on God, who raises the dead. And he did rescue
> us from mortal danger, and he will rescue us again.
> We have placed our confidence in him, and he will
> continue to rescue us.
>
> 2 CORINTHIANS 1:8-10, NLT

CHAPTER 2

CATCH YOUR BREATH

··

Joy delights in joy.
WILLIAM SHAKESPEARE

As a pastor, I've become pretty good at reading people's faces, especially right after a church service. Recently, I was shaking hands at the door when I saw a middle-aged woman with a scowl on her face approach me. I was already thinking, *This isn't good—she must've had a bad experience,* when she looked me in the eye and said, "Well, Pastor, I've found something I don't like about this church."

I kept smiling, pretending I wasn't discouraged to hear this. In fact, if I'm honest, I had already started thinking bad thoughts about her while at the same time saying, "Tell me what you don't like." In an instant her face changed and her scowl became a smile—she had been messing with me the whole time! She said, "The one thing I don't like about this church is that I have to wait six more days before I can come back!"

She went on to tell me how she'd been in church her whole life but had never enjoyed it until she found our church. She teared up a little as she described that going to church was now something she did out of delight, not duty. I asked her what this difference felt like, and her answer became the seed idea for this book: "It's like a breath of fresh air. It's like I can breathe again. This church has taken my relationship with God from the 'got to' to the 'get to.'"

FRESH BREATH

The apostle Paul, who regularly endured hostility and persecution, had even more reason than the woman in my church to be in the doldrums. His life as an evangelist was far from easy. So in the midst of life's storms and unending obligations, how did Paul find an environment that was both life-giving and life-changing?

In a little-known passage, Paul described one friend in particular as one who "refreshed" him. His name was Onesiphorus, and he was one of those obscure, behind-the-scenes guys you may never have heard of. The Greek word Paul used to describe this friend literally means "to put breath back in, to recover breath." It's as if Onesiphorus gave Paul emotional CPR, breathing encouragement and inspiration into his Christian brother. "May the Lord bless Onesiphorus and all his family, because he visited me and encouraged me often. His visits revived me like a *breath of fresh air*" (2 Timothy 1:16, TLB, emphasis mine).

Maybe you have a friend like that, someone who always manages to cheer you up and cheer you on, to offer support and friendship in tangible ways. I've been blessed to have more than one of these kinds of refreshing friends. One in particular stands out, and that's my father-in-law, whom we recently lost. Billy gave me advice and counsel in a way that always made me feel stronger, smarter, and more talented than I felt before I approached him. His friendship was something I could rest in, and time with him was something I came to depend on to recharge my batteries and renew my spirit.

People like Onesiphorus and my father-in-law, Billy, tend to have an enormous impact in subtle ways. Their enthusiasm, positive approach, and energy for loving other people breathe life into those around them and transform the entire environment. Even if you haven't experienced this kind of relationship firsthand, we've all sensed the difference between a place with fresh air and a place without it. Sometimes you notice it as soon as you walk into a room; other times, it doesn't reveal itself until after a few visits. But there's definitely something, some quality in these people and their attitudes, that can transform any environment into a magnetic, life-giving, enjoyable place to be.

> *Life-giving people make an enormous impact in subtle ways.*

THE X FACTOR

In a classroom, we sense immediately whether the teacher is fueled by a life-giving undercurrent of passion, or whether he is uninterested in the subject and the students he is teaching. The students can be the same; the room itself, the same; the textbooks and assignments, the same. But the teacher makes the difference between an engaging, exciting, you-love-being-there kind of class and a lifeless, boring, you-can't-stay-awake kind of class. Math has never been my best subject, and I made straight Cs in high school. But in college, I had an amazing teacher who made math fun to learn. I don't remember my grades—although I know they were higher than the ones I got in high school—but I do recall what he taught me and how much I enjoyed his classes.

At the office, it's the difference between an environment where everyone watches the clock and feels stifled and weary and one where the time flies by and everyone enjoys what they do and feels committed to working together as a team. It's the quality you see in the dedication and enjoyment people have in their roles, the spark in their eyes that shows they truly can't wait to get out of bed in the morning and go to work. Usually, there's a boss or supervisor who loves working with people so much that her positive attitude becomes contagious. People love working with her and for her so much that the work somehow seems easier, even enjoyable.

You also recognize this life-giving quality very quickly in some people's homes, and it has nothing to do with the size of their house or the stylishness of their interior decor. We've all been in small starter houses that overflowed with warmth and charm as well as luxurious mansions that were as cold and lifeless as a concrete slab. The people inside, of course, provide the unique quality that transforms a house into a home. A life-giving home has a welcoming, inviting, relaxing environment that makes you feel special, like you belong. The people seem genuine and down to earth, glad that you're there and eager to offer you their hospitality.

When a church has this life-giving factor, you sense it within the first visit. You sing the same songs, read the same Bible as in any other church, but there's something different about the atmosphere of the place. People are truly glad you're there and naturally eager to get to know you. They demonstrate compassion and humility and a passionate commitment to serve others that's remarkably refreshing and inspiring. They display a shared bond in strong friendships, life-giving marriages, and healthy families. The people respect and accept one another, help one another in crisis, and simply enjoy worshiping and fellowshiping together. They enjoy serving one another. There's a healthy sense of love and mutual admiration, a shared commitment to similar values, and an anchor of confident security in their faith. You want some of what they have!

Not long ago someone sent me a blog post written by Audrey, a member of our Riverchase campus. In it, Audrey describes the intangible quality that she and her husband noticed the first time they came to the church. I think she explains it just about as well as I ever could:

The minute I walked into the building something felt different . . . something actually felt right. People were packed like sardines in the sanctuary—standing room only—and these people were freely worshiping God through song and praise. The Holy Spirit blanketed this room and I could feel him . . . this must be home.[1]

Audrey and her husband, Chris, quickly connected with Blake Lindsey, the campus pastor, and became members of the church, as well as one of our small groups. They wanted more of this refreshing breeze, and just as important, they now contribute to this fresh-air environment themselves.

This mysterious "X factor" feels like the heartbeat of a relationship, a home, a business, a classroom, a church. It feels like a breath of fresh air, an energy-giving, life-breathing force that draws you in and inspires you, empowering you to be all that God made you to be. You know when it's there and you know when it's not there, but what is it? And more important, how can you get it?

You've likely experienced this mysterious quality at one time or another. You may link it to certain kinds of people and places, but it's usually hard to pin down. It's an intangible force that inspires you with energy and fills you with new breath. It causes you to grow in ways you could never achieve by yourself. Jesus talked a lot about these kinds of environments. In his parable about the sower and the seed, he told us that it's not the seed itself that makes the difference—not even the farmer or the sunlight or rain. The secret's in the soil.

SOIL SAMPLE

While I may not have the greenest thumb, surprisingly enough I do know a thing or two about soil. When I was thirteen, I got my first real job working in a nursery. The family-owned business included several greenhouses, an arbor, and acres of shrubs, bushes, flowers, and plants. I would show up after school and work two or three hours until the place closed. My dad had encouraged me to take this job, not because we needed the money but because he wanted me to develop a strong work ethic. He knew that taking care of living things would teach me a sense of responsibility like nothing else could.

I wasn't thinking about such mature matters when I was there, though. All I knew was that I liked getting paid to get dirty and be outside a lot of the time. Although I always did whatever needed to be done, my main job was looking after the plants in the green-houses—herbs, coleus, bonsai, cacti, begonias, succulents, and ferns, to name just a few. Many of these plants had been grown from seeds and required special attention.

One thing they all had in common, however, was soil and fertil-izer. It didn't take me long to realize that soil quality is the real secret to a healthy plant. If the soil itself was full of nutrients and life, the plant would grow incredibly fast. This made sense to me because I'd watched my grandmother make her own compost to fertilize her tomato plants and prize-winning rosebushes. Enriching the soil with living elements produced heartier plants. Water and light are important as well, but nothing grows if it can't take root by drawing nourishment from its surroundings.

Since most of us don't make our own compost like my grandma did, gardeners ensure that all the life-giving nutrients needed to pro-mote health are present in fertilizer and potting soil. When browsing the gardening center at your local nursery, you may have noticed that fertilizer labels have three bold numbers. The first number indicates the amount of nitrogen, the second refers to the amount of phospho-rus, and the third specifies the amount of potassium. So, for instance, a bag of 10-10-10 fertilizer contains 10 percent nitrogen, 10 percent phosphorus, and 10 percent potassium, the three main elements that virtually all plants need in order to grow.

WHERE YOU'RE PLANTED

That may be more than you wanted to know about horticulture, but this basic understanding helped me get a clearer picture of what Jesus was talking about in several of his parables. Many times he used farming and gardening metaphors to help people understand spiritual truth. In an arid, mostly desert land, the importance of things like water, shade, and good soil was something everyone understood.

For instance, Jesus said, "This is what the kingdom of God is like. A man scatters seed on the ground. Night and day, whether he sleeps or gets up, the seed sprouts and grows, though he does not know how. *All by itself the soil produces grain*—first the stalk, then the head, then the full kernel in the head. As soon as the grain is ripe, he puts the sickle to it, because the harvest has come" (Mark 4:26-29, emphasis mine). Notice that Jesus said that regardless of what the seed does, the plant is growing even if it really doesn't know how. It's not the farmer's efforts; it's not even the seed's efforts. It's the soil that makes the difference.

In another famous parable, Jesus talked about the consequences when the same kind of seeds land in different kinds of soils:

> Listen! A farmer went out to sow his seed. As he was
> scattering the seed, some fell along the path, and the birds
> came and ate it up. Some fell on rocky places, where it did
> not have much soil. It sprang up quickly, because the soil
> was shallow. But when the sun came up, the plants were
> scorched, and they withered because they had no root.
> Other seed fell among thorns, which grew up and choked
> the plants, so that they did not bear grain. Still other seed
> fell on good soil. It came up, grew and produced a crop,
> some multiplying thirty, some sixty, some a hundred times.
>
> MARK 4:3-8

Where the seeds landed clearly mattered. Some seeds never took root because they fell on the path and got eaten by the birds. Others landed in shallow soil and could not grow deep roots and consequently wilted when the sun scorched them. Some seeds grew in soil that was already supporting thorns, which choked the budding plants so that they could not bear their grain. Finally, some seeds fell on good soil and not only grew to produce a grain crop but thrived and multiplied.

I think most of us know what "breath of fresh air" environments look like but aren't sure how to create them or contribute to them.

The X factor is inside us. It's something we breathe in so that we can then breathe life wherever we're planted.

Based on Jesus' parable, the secret seems to lie in the soil. The soil produces grain all by itself, apart from the work of the farmer or anything else. In the same way, the X factor is inside us. It's something we experience, something we breathe in so that we can then breathe life wherever we're planted.

So what is it? How do we tap into it? How can we be like Onesiphorus and "refresh" those around us by bringing life everywhere we go? The first step is understanding more about what *it* is.

THE MAGNIFICENT SEVEN

When Craig Groeschel founded LifeChurch.tv, people were drawn there, sensing a powerful, life-changing force. In *IT*, his aptly named book, he defines what "it" is and how ministries can get and keep it. He writes, "*It* is not a model, a system, or result of programs. You can't purchase *it*. *It* can't be copied. Not everyone will get *it*. Even though *it* can't be taught, *it* can be caught."[2] I agree that we can't pin down exactly what produces this life-giving breath inside us, but I like to think we can understand it better by considering its attributes. Just as gardeners analyze soil to see what elements are present, we can evaluate the culture around us in hopes of catching this quality for ourselves.

In order to make the intangible more tangible, let's define *culture* as a combination of attitudes, values, and practices that characterize a person, group, organization, or institution. While numerous self-help books and leadership guides have been written about creating a life-giving culture—those attitudes, values, and practices that characterize a person or organization—one in particular had a huge impact on me and my ministry. Years ago, I read a book called *Natural Church Development* by Christian A. Schwarz that compiled and sorted the results of a study conducted in 70,000 churches on six continents.[3]

This study was designed as a tool to understand church health and growth patterns. Viewing the church as a living organism, the researchers weren't focused on numerical growth, but on improving the overall health of the church. Schwarz and his team established what they called a quality index, a sort of "soil sampling" of these thousands of churches. It was probably the most extensive study of church growth ever conducted.

When I first read through the study's findings, it occurred to me that if the elements of the quality index reflected health in churches, then they must also apply to individuals. After all, our church communities are made up of people from diverse backgrounds. If a church reflected healthy growth, then it had to have started with its members. I also suspected that if their findings applied to churches, they would also apply to homes, offices, classrooms, and boardrooms.

While there isn't a direct one-on-one correlation between Schwarz's eight characteristics and the ones I came up with, they definitely reflect one another. Based on their study, here's my summary of the seven qualities that produce health:

1. Enjoying your relationship with God; participating out of delight rather than duty
2. Embracing your uniqueness and the calling that God has on your life

3. Feeling empowered to be creative and pursue your dreams
4. Having a sense of purpose and focus, and living out this purpose every day
5. Laughing and finding humor in all areas of life
6. Developing life-giving relationships by addressing hurts, wounds, and disappointments as they occur
7. Focusing on others more than yourself

From day one I taught these principles in our church, since I was convinced that when believers embrace a culture of life, the church itself will become life-giving. Let's briefly consider each of these qualities and its importance in creating a breath of fresh air in your life.

ENJOYING GOD

Many people have never even dreamed that God is someone to be enjoyed. Growing up in church, I actually had some kind of warped belief that serving God was supposed to be painful and difficult—that if I endured the experience, that made it more holy. It's not true. Serving God, reading your Bible, praying, and going to church can and should be some of the most enjoyable things you do.

The primary way to enjoy your relationship with God is by experiencing his presence in your life right here, right now. Your relationship with him can't be something you inherited, felt obligated to try, or pursued for other people. He's not some distant, mythical figure coming out of ancient stories. He's the dynamic, living, eternal Creator, your loving Father who knew you before you were even born.

The way to enjoy your relationship with God is by experiencing his presence in your life right here, right now.

When you experience God's presence, you begin to know his power. Prayer becomes a communication lifeline to your all-powerful God. Your faith is actually lived out with commitment, fire, and enthusiasm. You want to serve him because you love him and know him. You're not obligated or living by a checklist or forced to work harder.

EMBRACING YOUR DESIGN

Scripture tells you that you have been fearfully and wonderfully made by God (Psalm 139). Through David's words, God is calling you to embrace the way you look, the way you act, and the way you express your gifts. Your design reveals your identity. If you don't grasp how special and significant you are, then you'll never understand how much your unique contribution matters.

Several years ago Robert Record, a medical doctor and member at Highlands, told me, "I went to medical school to be a pastor. I think I'm supposed to use medicine as a way to reach hurting people and present the gospel."

After he shared a bit more of his vision, I told him, "If you go find a building that can house that ministry, Highlands will buy it." And we did. We purchased a former county health department building in one of Birmingham's poorest communities. Today, about fourteen thousand patients receive medical care there each year. Christ Health Center fills a void created when the county clinic closed, since many area residents have no transportation and thus no way to get to facilities in other parts of the city.

Highlands operates the health center and the Dream Center next door, not because I thought it would be a good idea. Frankly, I didn't have the vision for these ministries at all. But I believe God placed Dr. Record and others like him at Highlands because he wanted our church to demonstrate his love to one of the neediest areas of our city.

I often say Highlands looks just like the people God sent to us. He has given our church the people we need to do what he has called us to do. Likewise, he has placed you where you are for a particular reason. In my humble opinion, no factor will bring you more joy than getting in touch with your unique gifts and abilities and then using them to serve others. However, to do so you must know who you are and where you fit in the body of Christ. There's no substitute for knowing your special identity as God's child.

FEELING EMPOWERED

Once you know who you are, you're only halfway there. In order to turn your vision into reality, you need to be in an environment where you feel empowered to live out your true identity.

Not too long ago I listened to a cassette of the first message I ever preached. I couldn't believe how bad it was. But when I delivered it, I thought I was doing pretty well—especially because I saw my pastor, who was sitting in the front row, scribbling notes as I spoke. The next day he took me out to lunch and pulled out his notepad. He'd filled page after page—not with insights from my sermon as I'd thought, but with his critiques. I was crushed, but after he gave me his input, he told me he wanted me to preach the following week too. He was determined to develop the potential in me and gave me a chance to grow into my gifting, raw as it was back then.

I've been so blessed to be around empowering leaders most of my life. My pastor, my dad, my coaches, and my teachers—they all made a huge difference in my life. They believed in me and saw the potential I couldn't yet see. Then they helped me focus and channel my abilities.

Environments where those over you don't see your potential become life-draining situations very quickly. On the other hand, empowering environments will challenge you to your core in an atmosphere of encouragement. They will allow you to try—and even fail—and just keep trying.

KEEPING FOCUS

In order to live a "breath of fresh air" life, you will have to eliminate events, activities, and relationships that don't contribute to who you are and what you're about. When you discover your identity and unique gifts and then become empowered to exercise them, you need to prioritize and focus on what matters most, those things you're called to do that no one else can do. Many people are going through life "out of breath" because they are involved in so many activities— many of which do not contribute to their life's purpose.

Several years ago, God gave me a vision to train, resource, and encourage pastors and church leaders who were struggling—those who felt they were not reaching their ministry potential. Our team at Church of the Highlands set a goal to help one thousand churches that had fewer than one thousand people in attendance break that barrier. After working with hundreds of churches over the past few years, we noticed one common problem resurfacing over and over again: the vision of the church was unclear. They had a vision state-ment, but most church leaders didn't really know what they were trying to accomplish. They didn't have a measurable win. And the ones who did were still putting a lot of energy into events and pro-grams that did not contribute to their purpose. What they needed was focus. And most saw immediate momentum restored to their ministry as soon as they put every idea, program, and budget request through the filter of their purpose.

As individuals, you and I need to use the same scrutiny when invited (or even begged) to commit to a new activity. You'll need to be intentional about focusing on the work God has called you to do and passing on the rest. So many agendas will compete for your energy and attention that if you're not committed to your own unique purpose, then your resources will be drained by everything else.

LAUGHING OFTEN

People and cultures that are life-giving know that nothing goes as planned. They don't expect life to be perfectly predictable and scripted. They know how to improvise and use unexpected challenges as opportunities for growth, for faith, and for humor. When you're willing to lighten up, nothing will be so important or serious that it blinds you to the many blessings and opportunities in your life. Even the most challenging situations can become fun. Laughter is like the secret spice in a Cajun gumbo that unites and brings out all the other flavors.

CULTIVATING RELATIONSHIPS

Most of us need a healthier view of relationships. We usually expect way too much from people. Often we judge them based on their actions even as we judge ourselves based on our intentions. We need God's grace and extravagant love in our lives in order to love and forgive others in life-giving ways. Otherwise, we become resentful, distrustful, or even cynical. Then our bitterness seeps out and poisons all our relationships.

You and I cannot be breath-giving, life-loving people if we have a poor view of others. We must cultivate our relationships in all areas in order for us to have the soft hearts needed to breathe—and receive—new life.

FOCUSING ON OTHERS

Over eighty of our church's small groups serve meals, tutor, or do maintenance and administrative work at our medical clinic and the Birmingham Dream Center. When a reporter asked Dr. Record about the Highlands members who serve in these ministries, he said, "Everybody has some sacred dream in them. If you get them serving, they're focused on a purpose that's something bigger than themselves."[4]

When you serve others, you will gain a new and broader perspective on your own needs and troubles. Praying for other people, providing for their needs, giving to missions, and celebrating changed lives creates a culture that makes others the reason you exist. When you look beyond yourself, you realize that "others" are a lot like you, that we share more similarities as people than differences. When people are your primary focus, new life enters and you experience more joy than you could imagine.

CATCH THE BREEZE

I'm convinced that all of us are capable of being this kind of person. That's what this book is all about. Maybe you've been in the doldrums or going through a slump in your life. Maybe you find yourself in a life-draining crisis or, more likely, just numb from going through the day in, day out routine of life. You get up, get the kids up and ready for school, go to work, chauffeur kids around for sports, go home, have dinner, clean up, look over a report for work, pay the bills, and finally collapse, exhausted, into bed so that you can do it all over again the next day.

Maybe there's some variety on those days when you throw in some overtime at work or meet with your small group from church. But it all blurs together, and you sometimes wonder why you do what you do. You're almost afraid to stop and step back and look closely at your life for fear of what you'll find. You don't even know if you're happy or if you're doing what you should be doing. You simply exist.

Our journey together in these pages is about reclaiming your life and breathing fresh air into all areas of it. You may feel like you're gasping for air and desperately need CPR. Or maybe you're at the top of your game, and like an elite athlete on the sidelines inhaling pure oxygen, you simply need refreshment before you reenter the competition.

Most likely you alternate between the two, some days feeling like you are on the verge of a complete breakdown and other days feeling like all you need is a short breather. Either way, we all long for that sweet sensation of opening a window and allowing a gentle breeze to caress us. No matter where we are on life's seas—in the doldrums, in a hurricane, or in calm waters—you and I need wind in our sails to move forward.

The strategies I offer in this book go beyond seven principles to a happier life. They're not more ideas on how to be a better Christian or guidelines for controlling your behavior. The internal combustion of personal passion requires something supernatural happening inside of you. It requires God's presence in your life in a real, tangible, feel-it-everyday kind of way.

And this means falling in love with him like never before.

BREATHING LESSON

The apostle Paul wrote Timothy about the friend who had refreshed him like a "breath of fresh air." If you long for your own Onesiphorous, begin to pay close attention to the source of any cool, refreshing breezes that are currently blowing in your life. As you do, you'll discover it's relatively easy to spot the difference between a person or place that pours life into you and one that drains you.

When did you most recently notice a person or place that brought you a "breath of fresh air"? What were the circumstances? How did this person or location refresh you? Once you are able to recognize the intangible qualities that invigorate you, you will find it easier to pursue their sources.

> Today I have given you the choice between life and
> death, between blessings and curses. Now I call on
> heaven and earth to witness the choice you make.
> Oh, that you would choose life, so that you and your
> descendants might live!
> DEUTERONOMY 30:19, NLT

CHAPTER 3

DO YOU LOVE ME?

···

God loves us the way we are, but too much to leave us that way.
LEIGHTON FORD

Like a lot of people in the Deep South, I grew up going to church every time the doors were open. I don't think I ever missed a Sunday in church in my life—ever. In addition to the two services on Sunday, we attended Wednesday night prayer meeting. But the Sunday morning services are what I remember best. My dad, the church organist, played the three-keyboard Wurlitzer on the right-hand side of the platform across from the pianist, Mr. McCutcheon, who was seated to the left of the pulpit. In her burgundy choir robe, Mom sang soprano in the church choir, which consisted of a couple dozen members.

From these vantage points, both my parents could keep their eyes on my siblings and me during the service. Sure, we whispered and giggled and pinched each other and chewed the gum that my grandmother would give us (even though Dad didn't like it), but we were always aware that if we got too loud (signaled by Dad looking over his shoulder in our direction), there was going to be some serious discussion when we got home.

Just because I spent all that time in church didn't mean I necessarily liked it. I knew it was probably good for me, like running wind sprints in gym class or eating brussels sprouts, but I assumed that meant I wasn't supposed to enjoy it. It was just what you did if you were a good family in Baton Rouge, Louisiana, in the seventies.

RELATIONSHIP NOT RELIGION

I never doubted God's existence or the need to trust Jesus to save me. As I got older, I prayed and read my Bible, and I often responded to the altar call at the end of the service. But even though I tried to learn more about God and the Bible and what Christians were supposed to do, I always felt that no matter how much time I put in, it was never going to be enough. Every time I went to church, I either heard about the things I shouldn't be doing that I was doing or I heard about the things I wasn't doing and needed to do.

This was the only approach I knew to having a relationship with God. I tried to please him by doing the right things and by not doing the wrong things. Sometimes I wondered if it was even worth it.

The truth is, I really didn't like church—and I didn't enjoy too many Christians. While they smiled, nodded, prayed, and said, "God bless you, brother," they seemed just as frustrated as I was underneath their good church faces. It was probably because they didn't want to be there either. Or at least that was my theory. I had so many questions. Why was it such a struggle to do everything right? How could I actually enjoy this so-called wonderful, joy-filled Christian life? And why, despite all my efforts to do everything right on the outside, did I still feel so empty, numb, and lifeless on the inside?

Since then I've discovered that when the focus is on doing spiritual things and avoiding sinful things, the motivation is all wrong.

That realization happened in my sophomore year of high school. By the time I turned fifteen, I had secretly checked out on God but still attended church every Sunday and went through the motions. Then a friend of mine invited me to a youth service at his church. The worship there was like nothing I had ever seen before. In some strange way, I was both attracted to it and scared to death at the same time. People seemed genuinely happy and excited, and they passionately praised God and worshiped. Not only that, but the youth pastor taught in a way that I understood and that seemed relevant to my everyday life.

When the focus is on doing spiritual things and avoiding sinful things, the motivation is all wrong.

I had never seen young people so in love with God. I couldn't believe it! This was so different than anything I'd ever experienced. I asked myself, *Is this real? Or is this some kind of cult? If this is who God really is, then I want to know him, love him, and follow him for the rest of my life.* When I got home I opened my Bible, determined to discover for myself what it really meant to be a Christian. I'm thankful the church I was raised in taught me enough about the Bible that I could search the Scriptures for myself.

I started with the Gospels, opening to the book of Matthew, and began reading. My goal was simple: to find out what the Bible says about how a person gets to heaven. And then it happened. The verses in Matthew 7 jumped off the page and answered my question—and it was completely different from anything I had ever heard before!

Not everyone who says to me, "Lord, Lord," will enter the kingdom of heaven, but only the one who does the will of my Father who is in heaven. Many will say to me on that day, "Lord, Lord, did we not prophesy in your name and in your name drive out demons and in your name perform many miracles?" Then I will tell them plainly, "I never *knew you.* Away from me, you evildoers!"

MATTHEW 7:21-23, EMPHASIS MINE

For the first time I realized that God wasn't keeping a checklist, marking down what I was doing and not doing. He just wanted to *know* me. My eternal destiny wasn't about religion but relationship. And so that December night in 1978—Christmas break of my sophomore year of high school—I gave my life to Jesus and told him that if he would give me another chance, then he would never find another person who would follow him with more passion than I would. It may sound clichéd, but truly, that night my life changed forever.

Five years later, at the age of twenty, I wound up on staff at the same church I had visited with my friend. After that night in December, I had fallen in love with God and had committed myself to him. I wanted to serve him, and it made sense to do it at the place where I first experienced such an alive, dynamic faith.

However, as I grew in my relationship with God and served in ministry, I discovered that I had a tendency to fall right back into the same spiritual numbness I felt before my conversion experience. When Tammy and I were still fairly new parents, I was serving as a youth pastor in Colorado Springs. Every morning I spent time in my little office in our basement, reading my Bible and praying. One morning after about a half hour down there, I heard Michael's and Sarah's footsteps as they ran squealing across the kitchen just above me. Their laughing voices made me want to run upstairs and join the fun.

Right then I got real honest with my heavenly Father. "God, I don't want to be down here right now. This is work, and I'd rather be upstairs playing with my kids. Why is that?"

I sensed God's voice telling me, "Because your relationship with them is different from the one you have with me."

"Lord, what do you mean?" I asked.

"You treat me so formal . . . everything is timed . . . everything is out of obligation. You don't even talk to me the same way you talk to them. What would it look like if you talked to me like you talk to them? What would it be like if you were just in love with me?"

It's difficult to describe the weight that was lifted off me once again. God was reminding me that I could either try to get closer to him by doing the right things and hoping it would "take" on the inside, or I could fall in love with him on the inside, knowing that everything would then happen naturally on the outside.

There seems to be something in our human nature that draws us away from a life-giving relationship with Jesus because it feels more comfortable to focus on what to do and not do. That tendency robs us of real joy and peace. As a young pastor trying to live up to people's expectations, I had fallen back into the pattern of trying hard to do everything perfectly—which I couldn't do, of course.

INSIDE OUT

I'm not alone in this struggle. Many people are still trying to reach God through religion. They're doing everything right on the outside and remain empty on the inside.

Maybe you're in the same boat—caught in the doldrums of wanting more and not knowing how to move forward. Here are a couple of indicators that you need some fresh air in your life. Symptom number one is that you're doing the right things but you don't enjoy them. This feeling goes beyond simple fatigue or occasional boredom to indifference. A subtle, unspoken sense of "what difference does this make?" creeps in. You may even feel a little guilty for not having the peace and joy that you once experienced or that you've heard someone who's in love with God should experience.

Something in our human nature draws us away from a life-giving relationship with Jesus because it feels more comfortable to focus on what to do and not do.

Another classic symptom is when you begin to envy others who seem to grow closer to God by doing what you've done. Doing the right thing seems to be working for everyone but you. As you look around at the people in your church or in your group of Christian friends, you notice that their efforts seem to be producing fruit where yours never have. You read the same books, go to the same small group, even do the same Bible studies, and yet your attempts remain dry, lifeless, uninteresting, and uninspiring.

This isn't just a twenty-first-century, American phenomenon. In every nation of the world and in every period of time you'll find people practicing liturgies, reciting prayers, and obeying traditions while their hearts are far from God. They desperately try to know God by doing the right things externally. Perhaps the problem is more prevalent in our world today, though. In our technologically advanced age, where every problem has a solution, every bad habit can be changed, and every flaw can be corrected, we still cannot reduce our relationship with God to a formula.

We get stuck in a mind-set that tells us that what we do on the outside is the end in itself. Don't get me wrong—it's good to do good things. We can't rely on our feelings as the engine to fuel our actions, just like a musician can't wait until she has inspiration to play, but must develop her talent by practicing every day. It's the internal motivation, the passion that fuels our desire, that determines whether or not our endeavor has breath.

But how can we tap into this spiritual passion within us? How can we cultivate our relationship with God and not get caught up in the performance trap of religion?

LOVE RULES

Answering this question has been the struggle of mankind since the Garden of Eden. From the very beginning of creation, people have always been given a choice. With Adam and Eve in the Garden, it was the choice of whether to eat from the tree of life or the tree of the knowledge of good and evil. Would they choose the fresh air of relationship with their Creator? Or the performance-only trap of external dead works?

We know what they chose and the chain reaction it set off for all humankind. But why did Adam and Eve make that choice? And why do we so often follow their example? I believe it's because we think it's easier to measure, to quantify, and to control our behavior when we have an external set of rules. When we have a checklist to work from, we can track our progress and know where we stand. Besides, relationships are messy.

And yet relationships are what we're made for, what we all crave on the inside. Most religious people are banking their salvation on what they do right and avoid doing wrong. As long as their behavior conforms to this standard, then they figure they're in the clear. They deserve to know God's favor, to live a prosperous and joyful life, and to go to heaven when they die. After all, they've done everything right, haven't they?

Probably one of the most surprising discoveries I've made while studying the Bible is that God does not condone religion. It's a consistent theme throughout Scripture. Religion is man's external effort to please God. But God doesn't care about all my efforts to get it right. He wants more, something far greater.

God does not condone religion.

In fact, this is one of the main issues Jesus confronted while on earth. He ignited a huge explosion within the religious establishment because he came and said, "I'm the Messiah, the Son of God. And you know what? Religion isn't the way to God."

THE CLASH

Most people think that Jesus came to bring about a religious order. Throughout history, people of all faiths have called Jesus a religious leader. I think he would have considered that description an insult.

Some of the strongest, harshest language Jesus ever used was aimed at the Pharisees and Sadducees, the Jewish religious leaders of his day. As we look at one of their confrontations, I think you'll see clearly that what God wants from them—and from us—is something much more than just obedience.

> Then some Pharisees and teachers of the law came to Jesus from Jerusalem and asked, "Why do your disciples break the tradition of the elders? They don't wash their hands before they eat!" Jesus replied, "And why do you break the command of God for the sake of your tradition? . . . You nullify the word of God for the sake of your tradition. You hypocrites! Isaiah was right when he prophesied about you: 'These people honor me with their lips, but their hearts are far from me. They worship me in vain; their teachings are but rules taught by men.'"
>
> MATTHEW 15:1-3, 6-9

Here it's clear that clean and unclean have nothing to do with germs and aloe-enriched hand sanitizer! The fundamental conflict was about what qualified a person to approach God. For the Pharisees, it was a matter of keeping their own external tradition of washing hands before they ate a meal. But Jesus quickly jumped to the heart of the matter—literally.

He responded to their superficial question about conformity with a profoundly unsettling question about their heart motives. And for reinforcement he referenced one of their own sources—Isaiah, a prophet they honored. Long before Jesus was born and began his ministry, it seems, people had decided they could give God lip service and remain just as self-centered and rebellious as they wanted on the inside.

Instead of focusing on knowing and loving God, their method became a matter of making and conforming to rules. They set themselves up to determine what was and wasn't holy and pleasing to God, often based on their own prejudices and self-righteous judgments.

They could feel superior about keeping all the rules they had made while condemning people who weren't doing the same. Their reliance on external regulations and obligations defined religion. God was kept at arm's length, or rather at heart's length, because they created their own rules.

When Jesus came along and clashed with the religious establishment, he was engaging in a battle that continues today. And as I see it, the crucial question comes down to this: how can we get to God? Or to back up a bit, how can we really know God? The way we know him is through worship—opening our hearts to him with honesty, sincerity, and humility. Jesus makes it clear that worship is relational, an internal posture of the heart, not a mechanical pose we can strike just for the sake of appearances. Others may not see the difference, but God knows our hearts and clearly knows the difference.

I DON'T KNOW YOU

Not only was Jesus direct in his confrontation with the religious establishment, he also reinforced the religion-relationship distinction in his teachings. He knew many people approached God through rules rather than relationship, banking their salvation on what they did rather than on who they knew. Understanding that sometimes the truth is more powerful when it sneaks up on us, Jesus often shared in parables, simple stories of illustration, that continue to intrigue us today.

> At that time the kingdom of heaven will be like ten virgins who took their lamps and went out to meet the bridegroom. Five of them were foolish and five were wise. The foolish ones took their lamps but did not take any oil with them. The wise, however, took oil in jars along with their lamps. The bridegroom was a long time in coming, and they all became drowsy and fell asleep.

At midnight the cry rang out: "Here's the bridegroom! Come out to meet him!" Then all the virgins woke up and trimmed their lamps. The foolish ones said to the wise, "Give us some of your oil; our lamps are going out."

"No," they replied, "there may not be enough for both us and you. Instead, go to those who sell oil and buy some for yourselves."

But while they were on their way to buy the oil, the bridegroom arrived. The virgins who were ready went in with him to the wedding banquet. And the door was shut.

Later the others also came. "Sir! Sir!" they said. "Open the door for us!" But he replied, "I tell you the truth, I don't know you."

MATTHEW 25:1-12

Notice that all the young women were virgins, which symbolizes their religious purity. Also notice that the foolish ones thought that the condition for eternal life was making sure they had done enough—that they had saved enough oil to light their path to go out and meet the bridegroom, a common wedding custom at the time. However, by relying on the issue of how much oil they had in their lamps, they missed the party!

The reason the bridegroom, representing Jesus himself, says that the foolish virgins can't come in has nothing to do with being a virgin or with having enough oil. He doesn't say, "Sorry, your lamps aren't lit so you can't come in." Nor does he say, "Whoops, I can only admit virgins to this celebration and, well, you don't qualify." No, the reason he cites for not allowing the foolish virgins to enter is simple: "I don't know you." It's a matter of intimacy, an internal matter of what is going on inside their hearts. All of heaven will be about our relationship with God, not our religion—those things we do on our own to try to gain his favor.

FORWARD MOTION

Maybe you already know the Lord, but the way you know him isn't working for you. You're not enjoying your relationship with him. Here's the real secret: you can fulfill the commands of the Bible better by falling in love with God than by trying to obey him. It's not that your obedience isn't significant or relevant; it's simply not the center of the wheel. No, the hub of your life is your relationship with God. Your behavior and obedience radiate like spokes from the center of your life and allow you to roll forward. When you try to make your external behavior the hub on which you turn, you get stuck. Forward motion must be fueled by love.

You can fulfill the commands of the Bible better by falling in love with God than by trying to obey him.

Some people try to be good by doing godly things—reading their Bibles, praying, and serving those in need. But they're doing these things out of a sense of religious duty and obligation, not because they're in love with God and want to know him and offer up their lives to him. Then they wonder why their spiritual lives are so dry. Aren't they doing everything a good Christian should do? Well, then, why isn't God coming through with his end of the deal? Why isn't he answering their prayers and giving them the abundant life of peace and joy that Jesus said he brought to us?

The Christian faith is not a business transaction. It's not an arranged marriage where you receive a dowry of riches for compliance. Christianity only works if you're in love. All relationships are enjoyable when you're in love.

If you are trying to fight temptations by working on self-control, you're working on the wrong thing. I'm all for living a disciplined life, but there's a better way. Temptation is a test of your *relationship,* not your self-control. Whether or not you pray does not depend on your self-control. It does, however, reveal your relationship with God. Do you really want to talk to God? And better still, do you want to listen and hear what he wants to say to you?

It's time to stop trying to please him and simply love him. Stop doing things out of obligation. Only do the things that enhance your relationship with him, the things that please you because they delight him.

It's funny, the things we do for love. I hate cleaning out the garage—the time, the effort, the trouble. Sure, the outcome is nice, but is that really how I want to spend a weekend? However, my wife feels like the most loved woman in the world when I help her clean out the garage or tackle a big project that needs to be done. It's better than sending her a dozen roses—well, almost. The point is, I do it because I love her so much that it brings me joy to do something I know she really appreciates.

What we do for God also reveals the extent of our love. Jesus said, "*If you love me*, you will obey what I command" (John 14:15, emphasis mine). For years I read that verse this way—"If you love me, you will obey me and prove how much you love me." But that's not what he says. He simply says that when we love him, our obedience to him will flow out of our relationship. I'm afraid that most of us don't grasp the enormous extravagance of our Father's love and the lengths to which he's willing to go to show it. That's why the apostle Paul prayed that we might know and understand God's love (see Ephesians 3:14-21).

When we love Christ, our obedience to him will flow out of our relationship.

One of my greatest revelations of God's love came when my firstborn son, Michael, was about two years old. My wife was attending a friend's baby shower and had taken Michael with her. She was sitting in a metal folding chair and didn't realize that Michael was hanging on the back of it. When she got up, Michael fell backward and pulled the chair right on top of him. The metal chair hit him on the bridge of his nose and cut it wide open. Minutes later, I got the call that my wife and son were on the way to the emergency room.

As the plastic surgeon began to sew up his nose, Michael screamed, "Daddy, please—help me, Daddy." All I could do was watch as the surgeon finished his work. I would have done anything to take my son's place on that table. On the way home from the hospital, while Michael slept in the car seat, I cried uncontrollably. And in that moment, God spoke to me: "That's the way it felt for me when my Son was on the cross—but I let it happen because I love you, Chris." I realized then how great the Father's love is for me. The fact that he allowed his Son to go through such pain for me—and for you—is overwhelming.

DO YOU LOVE ME?

Recently, I was struck by what it means to have love—rather than tradition, obligation, or manipulation—at the center of your relationship with someone. Channel surfing one night, I caught an old favorite, the musical *Fiddler on the Roof*. I remember seeing it in high school and enjoying the insight into Jewish life and customs and the way the story depicted the clash between tradition and change.

You might recall that Tevye, a traditional Jewish patriarch, and his wife, Golde, have five daughters. Set in Russia at the dawn of the twentieth century, the story explains the custom of allowing a matchmaker to pair a single young Jewish woman with a desirable husband. As Tevye's daughters rebel against this practice and insist on marrying for love, Tevye must wrestle not only with tradition, but also with a far more personal crisis.

Tevye and Golde have been married for over twenty-five years, and like everyone else they know, their wedding was arranged by a matchmaker. In light of their daughters' revolt in the name of love, Tevye asks his wife a crucial question in the song, "Do You Love Me?" At first, Golde dismisses his question as silly. After all, she points out, hasn't she always done everything he's ever asked of her? Hasn't she been a good wife?

But Tevye explains that there's a difference between loving someone for who he or she is and the bond you share on the one hand, and submission through traditional obligation on the other. Once he makes the distinction clear for her, Golde admits that she does indeed love him now, even if that was not what had first brought them together. Their relationship illustrates the contrast between religion and relationship with God in a beautiful way.

Falling in love with God is just like falling in love with another person. You think about him constantly and want to be with him all the time. You can throw away your checklists and just enjoy spending time together. Your only desire is to be with him, to enjoy him, to receive what he wants to give you, and to give him everything you have. Like Tevye's song to Golde, I believe God continues to whisper to each one of us: "Do you love me?"

SHOW YOUR LOVE

It's no wonder so many people don't enjoy their Christian faith when all they know is obligation and duty-motivated obedience. If you're serious about catching the refreshing breeze of God and moving forward, then you have to keep your love for God alive. Don't just try to keep it on life support by relying on your religion. That will keep you grounded in the doldrums.

Jesus offers you something far better: he invites you to fall in love with him, to know who he really is and not just who others say he is. "You are the giver of life. Your light lets us enjoy life" (Psalm 36:9, NCV). That is the key to finding ultimate fulfillment in life. Foster your relationship in a way that deepens your intimacy. Fall more in love with him. Discover more of who he is. Enjoy the fullness of who he is as your Lord, your Father, your Creator. This is the fundamental message of the Bible, and yet I often fear that so many have missed it.

People end up viewing Christians as indentured servants to a divine tyrant who demands "good behavior" from his followers. Again, they get a negative impression of what it means to have faith in a loving God. They don't see us enjoying a divine romance and instead often interpret what they see as something negative or even abusive. But God is the essence of love, the reason we can even attempt to love others. If we ever stop loving God, then it's over "because no one can eat or enjoy life without him" (Ecclesiastes 2:25, NCV).

God invites us into the masterpiece of his love, his character, and his personality directly. It's the key to our ultimate fulfillment in life. Rather than trying to obey a checklist, when we cultivate a relationship with God, then it's no big deal to obey his commands. We want to please him, to know him, to trust him.

In chapter 1, we exposed the lifeless condition we all can find ourselves in from time to time. And in chapter 2, we explored what fresh air looks like. But before we can start the process of breathing again, it's critical to realize that it all begins with a vibrant, intimate relationship with God.

Over the years, I've watched discouraged believers—myself included—finally experience the fresh wind that pushed them out of the doldrums when they addressed one or more of the eight areas we'll look at in part 2. Each of these attitudes and actions has the potential either to draw us closer to God or move us away from him.

I hope you're convinced by now that a breath of fresh air doesn't come by changing anything on the outside. It doesn't come from formulas, systems, or structures. It comes when something happens on the inside of us, when our love for God is so vibrant that it spills over into the way we see everything.

As we will explore in the chapters to come, discovering love at the heart of our relationship with him breathes new life into every area of our lives, beginning with our perspective and outlook.

BREATHING LESSON

The Christian faith is not an impersonal business transaction. And Christianity will breathe life into you only if you have an intimate, personal relationship with God. While there are steps you can take to grow closer to God (as you'll see in coming chapters), your motivation has to be a desire for relationship, not a sense of duty. You can fulfill the commands of the Bible better by falling in love with God than by trying to obey a checklist of rules.

So the question is simple: Are you in love with God? Just like Tevye in *Fiddler on the Roof*, God is asking you, "Do you love me?" I encourage you to respond to his great love today.

Start by having an honest conversation with God. Tell him how you feel and where you're frustrated or afraid of loving him. Spend at least a few minutes listening for his response, perhaps while reflecting on the passage below.

> Christ will make his home in your hearts as you trust in him. Your roots will grow down into God's love and keep you strong. And may you have the power to understand, as all God's people should, how wide, how long, how high, and how deep his love is. May you experience the love of Christ, though it is too great to understand fully. Then you will be made complete with all the fullness of life and power that comes from God.
>
> EPHESIANS 3:17-19, NLT

PART 2

BRINGING FRESH AIR INTO YOUR LIFE

CHAPTER 4

EYES ON THE ETERNAL

You can't take it with you, but you can send it on ahead.

RANDY ALCORN

At Christmastime, I love buying presents for my kids. I get so excited trying to find a special present for each one of them—something not on their list, something that reflects their unique personality and personal interests.

Some selections are easier than others. My youngest son, Joseph, loves anything that's remote controlled—cars, planes, robots, you name it. Last year I was traveling home from Sydney, Australia, right before Christmas and saw something in the airport that I knew Joseph would absolutely love. Outside one of the shops, a guy stood demonstrating a remote-controlled toy helicopter. It flew with amazing precision, darting through the air above our heads, swooping down, and zooming back and forth throughout the terminal.

The salesman saw me watching and asked if I wanted to try the remote. Instead I held my hand above my head, palm up, and said, "Put it right here!" He smiled and sent the helicopter in my direction but took the long way. Back into the store and back out again, up above the escalators and then back toward me, where it hovered directly overhead before coming to a perfect landing on my palm.

Needless to say, I was hooked. The copter cost way more than I wanted to pay, but I was so excited thinking about Joseph playing with it that I didn't mind. Truth be told, I was looking forward to playing with it myself!

Now, buying Christmas presents for kids is always a risk. There's the risk that you're more excited about the gift than they are. There's nothing worse than watching them open the box, look up, and give you a courtesy smile before quickly setting it aside and moving on to the next package. Or spending an enormous amount of money on a gift only to find them playing in the box it came in minutes later.

I was pretty confident that I had a gift that would not receive either of those responses. And, sure enough, when Joseph opened my present, he was shocked and elated. He ran over and hugged me like it was the best gift he'd ever received. Score one for Dad! He loved it so much that he couldn't wait to get it out and try it. "Gently, gently," I kept cautioning as he ripped into the box to retrieve it. With the remote loaded with new batteries, he ran out the door with me not far behind. I told him to make sure he was in the middle of our cul-de-sac before starting the copter's inaugural flight—I even made him repeat my instructions back to me.

But in two seconds—his feet were barely out the door—the helicopter not only had liftoff but was stuck on top of our house! I'm not much of a fix-it guy and didn't even have an extension ladder to climb up on the roof. So I grabbed a fishing pole from the garage in hopes that I could hook it and lower it down. Well, I hooked it all right, and then proceeded to drag it to the edge of the roof, where the rotor blades caught on the gutter and abruptly snapped into pieces. Its maiden voyage was its last, and I was so disappointed.

WHAT DO YOU EXPECT?

Sometimes we're so excited about something in our lives that there's no way it can live up to our expectations.

Like my Christmas day disappointment, have you ever built up your expectations only to discover that things didn't work out the way you had hoped? There's nothing like unfulfilled expectations to take the wind out of your sails. Or as Scripture puts it, "Hope deferred makes the heart sick, but a longing fulfilled is a tree of life" (Proverbs 13:12). When you expect something and envision it a certain way only to discover that it's not that way at all, it really does feel like your heart becomes sick. But if you ever find something real and substantial, something solid that fulfills you, then it lives and breathes and grows inside you just like a tree of life.

For most of us, however, it's easier to become cynical and quietly desperate as our hope dries up with each unmet expectation in life. We end up feeling powerless to change ourselves, our circumstances, or other people. We hate ourselves for even wanting more or daring to hope that we might get what we long for. Unfortunately, even when we get what we wanted, it's never enough.

King Solomon, the son who followed in his famous father David's footsteps, was perhaps the most successful man who ever lived. He was world renowned for his incredible wisdom, and he had enormous wealth and a thousand wives.

Even though he thought those things would bring him fulfillment, all of it became meaningless to him. It even brought him to a place of depression and hating his life.

> I denied myself nothing my eyes desired; I refused my heart
> no pleasure. My heart took delight in all my work, and this
> was the reward for all my labor. Yet when I surveyed all
> that my hands had done and what I had toiled to achieve,
> everything was meaningless, a chasing after the wind;

nothing was gained under the sun. . . . So I hated life, because the work that is done under the sun was grievous to me. All of it is meaningless, a chasing after the wind.

ECCLESIASTES 2:10-11, 17

I love the way the book of Ecclesiastes describes an unfulfilled life with raw honesty. I'm convinced that it's one of the most relevant, practical books in the Bible for us today. Like Solomon, we often find ourselves in the midst of incredible abundance—a good family, a nice home, a great job, plenty of food and drink, and more clothes than we'll ever wear. And yet, we still find ourselves in the doldrums, stuck in place, going through the motions, and uncertain about how to break free to an authentic life filled with joy and purpose.

One of the reasons I find Ecclesiastes so comforting is that it gives voice to our feelings and describes the barriers that seem to lock us in place and prevent us from experiencing fulfillment in life. Right off the bat, Solomon expresses his frustration with his life and asks a question that many of us have asked at the end of a long workday. "'Everything is meaningless . . . completely meaningless!' What do people get for all their hard work under the sun? . . . The earth never changes" (Ecclesiastes 1:2-4, NLT). Some days it feels like nothing we do matters. And if nothing matters, then why bother? Why make the effort?

Of course, everyone has days like that. I feel that way, at least briefly, just about every Monday. Thinking back over our services the day before, I'm bound to ask myself, *Now why did I say that?* or *Why did I put that song there?* Then there are the times when I've been in the middle of a message series on parenting—at a time when my own teenager isn't speaking to me. Those are typical job hazards of a pastor, I guess. Yet if I focus only on what I and those around me can see, I get moored in the doldrums pretty fast.

When we experience enough of these days, they begin to have a cumulative effect on our souls. We feel like we're on a treadmill with no hope of getting off and moving forward. "The sun rises and the sun sets. . . . The wind blows. . . . Around and around it goes, blowing in circles. Rivers run into the sea. . . . Then the water returns again to the rivers and flows out again to the seas. Everything is wearisome beyond description" (Ecclesiastes 1:5-8, NLT). The cycle seems to continue, over and over again, with nothing changing as we go through the motions of each season. Too often life just wears us out, and no amount of sleep can relieve the weariness we carry inside.

At such times, nothing seems to bring much relief anymore, not sleep or new clothes or another vacation. We experience the law of diminishing returns. What we hoped would bring us joy isn't cutting it anymore. "No matter how much we see, we are never satisfied; no matter how much we hear, we are not content. History merely repeats itself" (Ecclesiastes 1:8-9, TLB). We feel trapped in the lives we've chosen, contained by the sum of our choices in life. The old saying "Be careful what you wish for—you might get it" stings us with the reality that our lives feel empty even after we have all that we thought we wanted.

DON'T LOSE HEART

While it's comforting on one level to have Solomon articulate our worries and offer a rant that's as timely as any blog entry today, we're still left feeling stuck.

For the substance of real hope that we long for, I believe we must look at someone whose life contrasts with Solomon's in almost every way. The apostle Paul was at the opposite end of the social, economic, and political spectrum from his poetic predecessor, yet he was clearly far more fulfilled in his life.

With no real personal possessions, certainly no permanent home or accumulated wealth, Paul thrived in the windblast of God's Spirit and sailed the adventure of a lifetime. Being shipwrecked and imprisoned, beaten and belittled, the guy never lost sight of his first love, and this passionate commitment grounded him regardless of his circumstances. He wrote:

> Therefore we do not lose heart. Though outwardly we are
> wasting away, yet inwardly we are being renewed day by day.
> For our light and momentary troubles are achieving for us
> an eternal glory that far outweighs them all. So we fix our
> eyes not on what is seen, but on what is unseen, since what
> is seen is temporary, but what is unseen is eternal.
>
> 2 CORINTHIANS 4:16-18

Paul never lost heart and neither should we. Why? Because what we see and experience around us is not all there is. Solomon grasped at all the pleasures the world offered and ended up in despair. Paul tossed aside everything he possessed in favor of loving Christ and ended up with eternal riches—and an appreciation for God's master plan.

At the beginning of this book, I shared my struggle with depression during a watershed year for me and my faith. Even when I was on vacation or engaged in one of my favorite hobbies, I'd often ask myself, *Really? Is this it?* But then God answered in a very real and personal way. He showed me what's real and reminded me that this is indeed not all there is. In fact, there is so much more than we can see!

After that year ended and I had moved on, I developed what I call my "problems theory" about the way life works. It's pretty simple, actually. My theory is that our problems never go away. If you or I solve one, another just pops up in its place. Like dandelions in your yard—or those Whac-A-Mole games at carnivals—one problem is resolved just as another one pops up. You find the money to pay for the car repairs and then the fridge goes out. You finally get the job transfer you've wanted for years, and then the company starts downsizing. As Solomon said, there always seems to be something waiting to undermine our contentment.

THE NEXT BIG THING

That leads me to the conclusion of my theory: if we want to enjoy life in the vibrant, fully alive way that we all crave, then we must have something to focus on that is bigger than our problems. When we have a larger perspective, we realize our problems are really not significant in the long run. Ten years from now, are we going to remember why we're mad at our best friend or how much it cost to pay the late fee on this month's mortgage payment?

If we want to enjoy a vibrant, fully alive life, we must have something to focus on that is bigger than our problems.

And if our problems *are* bigger and more life-consuming than those examples, we have all the more reason to recognize that God and his purposes are bigger. When we have cancer or lose our job or get divorced or have sick kids, we wonder how we'll get through it. The only way is to fix our eyes on something beyond our pain.

Once again, I look to the apostle Paul to show us how to do this. He wrote 2 Corinthians after going through many trials in Ephesus. He touched on those trials in the first chapter of his letter:

> We think you ought to know, dear brothers and sisters,
> about the trouble we went through in the province of Asia.
> We were crushed and overwhelmed beyond our ability to
> endure, and we thought we would never live through it. In
> fact, we expected to die.
>
> 2 CORINTHIANS 1:8-9, NLT

If anyone had a reason to wallow in his problems, it would seem to be Paul, who was staring death in the face. And yet he was able to look beyond his troubles. He continued:

> But as a result, we stopped relying on ourselves and learned
> to rely only on God, who raises the dead. And he did rescue

us from mortal danger, and he will rescue us again. We have placed our confidence in him, and he will continue to rescue us. And you are helping us by praying for us. Then many people will give thanks because God has graciously answered so many prayers for our safety.

2 CORINTHIANS 1:9-11, NLT

Paul was focusing on what was happening *in* him, not *to* him. Likewise, we can be sure that when something is happening to us, God is doing something in us—something that will shape us for eternity.

When my daughter, Sarah, was a toddler, it didn't take much for her to cry. She was a tender little girl, so it was sometimes hard to gauge the seriousness of what had happened based on her response to it. One day she came in crying very loudly and dramatically, and I came running. She'd scraped her knee. Other than being a little red, her knee seemed okay, but she just kept sobbing.

So I comforted her, put a Band-Aid on the hurt knee, and wiped away her tears, only to see them replaced by more. Then, inspired, I went over to our cookie jar and produced an orange Tootsie Pop. She immediately stopped crying and directed her attention toward the treat in my hand. Something had come into view that was bigger than her pain.

In the same way, the secret to living life with wind in your sails is to focus on more than your own problems and pain. Regardless of what's going on around you, look beyond yourself. Fix your eyes on the eternal—in every area of your life. What are you looking at when you think about where you are in your life right now? Could it be that your problems are not your real problem? Maybe you just have the wrong focus.

Maybe you're expecting from this life what can only come from God. Maybe you're expecting to receive from other people what only

God can give. Maybe you're expecting possessions and experiences to fulfill you in deep ways that only God can touch.

You and I need to get our focus off this life, off what we receive from other people, beyond what we own or see in front of us. We must constantly remind ourselves that the only things that matter are eternal things. The secret of life is to keep our focus there. This truth then leads to the question, how do we live so that our focus remains on eternity?

EYES ON THE PRIZE

Paul encouraged us to take a different position from the one most of us usually choose. "Since, then, you have been raised with Christ, set your hearts on things above, where Christ is, seated at the right hand of God. Set your minds on things above, not on earthly things" (Colossians 3:1-2). He exhorted us to look up with both our hearts and our minds so we can see beyond "earthly things" and focus instead on "things above."

Too many times we pray and basically try to bring God down to earth to do our bidding. It's kind of funny, really, like God doesn't already know what's going on in our lives. Like he needs us to fill him in on what needs doing, as if we're giving him some divine honey-do list. The purpose of prayer is not to inform God what needs to be done on earth; the purpose of prayer is to align ourselves with his realities in heaven. Prayer is not him coming down—he's already here with us through his Spirit. Prayer is about us being lifted up; it's choosing to look up and beyond, choosing to yield to his ways and not begging like a spoiled child for our own desires to be fulfilled.

This kind of prayer, this kind of refocusing our attention on eternal things, requires practice and patience. When we become too earthly minded, we usually end up dissatisfied and desperate, aware of the frustration that Solomon expressed about the limitations of life as we know it. We must learn to focus on heaven and pray, "Your kingdom come, your will be done, on earth as it is in heaven," just as Jesus instructed us in the Lord's Prayer.

Maybe I'm old-fashioned, but I think our grandparents understood this principle. They didn't expect to have everything they wanted like we often do today. They seemed to display contentment and gratitude that transcended their circumstances and life's losses. So many of the old songs they loved were about heaven. "When we all get to heaven, what a day of rejoicing that will be!" Or, "Some glad morning when this life is o'er, I'll fly away." Singing these hymns helped them refocus regularly on the reality of eternity.

My grandfather often talked about heaven and about how he longed to be reunited with our relatives "already invested on the other side." He envisioned something that filled him with a peace and a joy that didn't rely on what kind of car he drove, where he lived, or even the condition of his health. He knew that there was more to this life than material comforts and sensual experiences.

PRAYER FORCE ONE

Another way to get a heavenly focus in our lives is to mix prayer with worship. Both prayer and worship change our view of reality by expanding our awareness of God's presence and reminding us to look beyond what we can see with our eyes. When we worship, we often begin with our world feeling so big and all-consuming and God seeming so small and in the distance of our lives. Yet after we've worshiped, our perspective has righted itself and we realize just how big he is and how small we are. When we practice fasting, we experience the ultimate separation from the world and focus singularly on him.

When my dad first told me that he had cancer, I was devastated. I relied on his support and wisdom, and I couldn't imagine life without him. I went into my office, closed the door, and listened to worship music. Fifteen minutes later I emerged, still sad, but with the hope that comes from having an eternal perspective. I had been reminded that my God is big and my world is small.

Please understand that I'm not encouraging you to focus on some kind of emotional placebo that makes you forget about your worries. God definitely cares about your concerns. But I've found that he often has an easier time revealing his solutions when you and I are concentrating on his ways instead of our own. From my own experiences, I've learned that God tends to be very practical in helping us find solutions bigger than our own perspective permits.

Several years ago I was reading the Birmingham newspaper and saw that our city was one of the top ten most violent cities in America. Right there, in my own backyard, I discovered we were experiencing some of the worst crimes imaginable. I knew we had to get involved, but I wasn't sure how. Because we believe the root of such problems is spiritual, I immediately went to Mark Hand, our church's prayer coordinator, and told him we had to do something about this.

God often has an easier time revealing his solutions to our problems when we are concentrating on his ways instead of our own.

As a result of our prayers and conversations, we developed a strategy to systematically walk around our city in the highest crime areas and pray. A pickup truck with speakers in the back playing worship music led the procession. On our prayer walks, we asked for God's presence, protection, and provision. We immersed the city in our prayers that God's Kingdom would reign where hell seemed to be bursting to life. We wanted our earth to be invaded by heaven.

Our chief of police, himself a former pastor, found out about our prayer walks and supported us by giving us police escorts while we walked and prayed. Other churches joined us each third Saturday of the month. The experience was unbelievable! Hundreds gathered each month for an hour-long prayer walk. Many people from our church also began to serve this community through projects like mentoring schoolkids and refurbishing homes. For the past three years, we have seen a double-digit decline in almost every category of crime. Credit also goes to our city leaders and the police force for their hard work and vision. But God has answered our prayers and changed our city!

SERVICE WITH A SMILE

Focusing on others and their needs also helps restore our perspective. When we're serving others, we're no longer obsessing about our own problems and the painful realities that may accompany them. Serving is one of the most eternal things we can do, one of the things we do that matters most. When we're addressing the needs of others and making their needs a priority over our own, we realize that our problems aren't as big as they sometimes seem. Jesus said, "Do not work for food that spoils, but for food that endures to eternal life" (John 6:27).

At our church, the individuals on our Dream Team use their gifts to serve others in our church and the community beyond. Whether it's painting rooms at the children's hospital, providing child care for single moms, or leading a Bible study at a nursing home, these people look for ways to help people experience the love of God.

Recently I talked with a guy who serves at one of the state prisons where our Sunday services are broadcast every week. He told me that he had been in church his whole life, but it was just not that important to him. He came to Highlands and rededicated his life to Christ a few months ago and started serving on the Dream Team. With tears in his eyes, he said that his faith has become so real because he knows he is being used by God to reach the inmates in prison. Serving them gives him something to focus on, pray for, and live for.

I've found that the best way to pastor people is not always to focus on their individual needs but to focus people on the needs of others. There's nothing more satisfying than knowing that we've made a positive difference, an eternal difference, in the lives of other people. If we want to experience a breath of fresh air, we need to be in an empowering environment. When we discover the gifts that God has placed inside us and exercise them by serving others, it's almost like we give ourselves that hit of pure oxygen that a winded athlete receives on the sidelines of a big game.

I've found that the best way to pastor people is not always to focus on their individual needs but to focus people on the needs of others.

Another way to focus on serving others is to practice generosity. By being a giver and not always a taker, we use our resources for eternal purposes. Giving is one of the most eternally significant ways we can serve. We're called to be stewards, not hoarders, of what God has given us. We can't take it with us, so we'd better send it on ahead. "They share freely and give generously to those in need. Their good deeds will be remembered forever. They will have influence and honor" (Psalm 112:9, NLT).

Keep in mind, I'm not talking about tithing here—the tithe is the Lord's up front and off the top. We're not giving when we tithe; that is just a test to see if we will return what already belongs to God. No, I'm talking about living a generous life—giving our time, talents, and treasure away for no other reason than to bless others with God's love in hopes of making an eternal difference.

Every year our church gives out little business card–sized cards to our congregation that read, "A little something extra to show you God loves you." We tell people to take handfuls of them and show the love of God in practical ways—such as by paying for the order of the people in the car behind them in the fast-food drive-thru line and then asking the clerk to give those people the little card and tell them that the car ahead of them already paid for their meal. Some of our people leave a card with an especially generous cash tip for a waitress or waiter. Others buy something they know someone else needs, such as back-to-school supplies, and leave them anonymously with the little card.

Every year, we receive hundreds of calls, e-mails, and letters from people whose lives were blessed. We got a call from a lady who was given one of the cards at a fast-food restaurant drive-thru. She said that she had every intention of taking her own life once she got home that day. She had stopped to get her "final meal" before she went home to commit suicide, and then someone ahead of her paid for her meal and left the card. Surely that woman's life was worth so much more than the six bucks someone paid for her dinner! And I'm sure once the person who had bought her lunch heard the story, his or her problems suddenly seemed a whole lot smaller. We gain a new perspective on our own problems when we focus on the needs of others.

TRAVELING LIGHT

Finally, the most significant thing we can do, the thing with the most eternal impact, is to share the Good News of Jesus with someone. We can be a part of altering another person's eternal destiny. Knowing that heaven and hell are real, and knowing the scope of God's love and forgiveness, we should be sharing this ultimate breath of fresh air every opportunity we get. We should do it naturally and honestly, not in a way that feels contrived or pushy or artificial. But we should share our faith with a sense of urgency.

I was reminded of this recently when flying home from a conference on Southwest Airlines. While I was making casual conversation with the woman sitting next to me, she asked me what I did for a living. I told her that I was a pastor and she said, "Duh, we're all passengers."

"No," I said, "a pastor . . . like at a church." Well, I soon discovered that she didn't like church, and, of course, being me, I couldn't resist trying to change her perspective on what it means to know Jesus. I challenged her not to let past experiences define her faith journey. I mentioned to her that our church had online services and encouraged her to watch the live service that week because I'd give her a shout-out.

Before I delivered the message that Sunday, I welcomed the online audience and gave this woman a personal greeting. The following week she sent me an e-mail addressed to "Pastor/Passenger Chris" in which she thanked me for the shout-out as well as for taking time during the flight to explain to her how she could make her relationship with God personal. "So simple," she said, "yet no one has ever explained it that way." Learning of her new openness and desire to grow closer to God made my day.

I share this woman's response simply to show you what sharing our faith can look like in everyday life. I didn't hand her a tract or ask her to repeat a prayer after me. All I did was have a conversation with her. I was just myself. In some ways, it would have been easier to remain quiet and anonymous, another passenger on a crowded flight. I could have focused on my own comfort and tried to take a nap. I could have worried about what problems waited for me at home and at church. But I want to make as much of an eternal difference as possible, so when I can strike up a conversation with someone, I don't shy away from talking about my faith. If they find out I'm a pastor and that leads us into discussing spiritual things, then so be it.

BREATHING LESSON

One of the best ways for us to begin breathing fresh air again is by refocusing our lives on all that really matters—the eternal things. When we live for eternity, our difficulties don't disappear—but they don't weigh us down either. We can choose to focus on our problems even as we try to reach some imaginary place of trouble-free living. Or we can focus on eternal things and enjoy the fresh breeze of joyful purpose. Live for eternity, and you'll never live another day unfulfilled.

God calls us to travel light by keeping our destination in sight. Spend some time today asking yourself, *What am I currently doing that will have an eternal impact? What do I need to spend less time doing in order to focus more on the eternally significant goals to which God calls me?* Your responses to these questions will make a huge difference for all of eternity—one way or another. Don't miss out on the purpose for which God created you. Keeping your eyes on eternity will change the way you see everything.

> Let us throw off everything that hinders and the sin that so easily entangles, and let us run with perseverance the race marked out for us. Let us fix our eyes on Jesus, the author and perfecter of our faith.
>
> HEBREWS 12:1-2

CHAPTER 5
ATTITUDE ADJUSTMENT

....

Attitude is a little thing that makes a big difference.
WINSTON CHURCHILL

The most life-giving, breath-filled person I've ever known was my father-in-law, Billy Hornsby.

Billy gave his heart to the Lord in 1972 after a coworker encouraged him to read the Bible. Raised as a Catholic, Billy had never really read the Scriptures before, but when he did the Bible came alive and he gave his heart to Jesus. Three years later, Billy and his family moved to West Monroe, a small town in north Louisiana where he was stationed with the State Police. His CB handle was "Reverend Smokey." Billy was so on fire for the Lord that when he pulled truckers over for speeding, he would also share the gospel with them. He always kept copies of the book of John in his police car to hand out to speeders. He called them his "captive audience."

Billy had a huge burden for Europe, and in 1984 he moved his whole family to Germany to plant and support churches all across the continent. That's where I met Billy. I was a youth pastor in Baton

Rouge, and when I brought teams of students to Germany for summer missions, Billy and his family would host us. That's when I fell in love with Billy. You were probably thinking I was going to say that's when I fell in love with his daughter Tammy, but the truth is I never even thought about Tammy until one day when the Hornsby family was back home in the United States for a short break.

Billy had taken me out to eat at Phil's Oyster Bar on Government Street in Baton Rouge. He asked me what I thought about his oldest daughter, Tammy, and he encouraged me to take her out on a date so I could get to know her. I always say that was the day Billy proposed to me. He always told me that many were called, but few were chosen, and that God had spoken to him about me. So Tammy and I started dating, and at the end of every date, when I would take Tammy home, she would go to bed, but Billy and I would stay up for hours playing pool, talking, and dreaming big dreams for ministry.

To be honest, I still wasn't that interested in Tammy because she was so shy and called me "sir" since I was a pastor on staff. After a few months, Billy and the family went back to Germany, and just before they left, he told me that if I decided I couldn't live without Tammy I should give him a call.

After months of letters and phone calls to her in Germany, I realized that I couldn't live without her. Tammy is the sweetest person I've ever met. I like to say she could teach the sun to be more consistent because her loyalty, concern, and good nature never fluctuate. I actually flew to Germany with a ring and proposed to Tammy there. Thank goodness she said yes. That's a long way to go to hear a no!

LIVE LIKE YOU'RE DYING

In 2009, Billy discovered a small sore on the bottom of his foot. At first doctors told him that it wasn't anything to be concerned about. But when it wouldn't heal, the doctor decided to do a biopsy and found a stage 5 melanoma tumor on the bottom of his foot. The prognosis wasn't good, but Billy wasn't worried. He knew that God could heal him—and if God didn't, he said, "I've already lived an incredibly full life—better than I ever hoped or dreamed."

In all his struggles through life, Billy never complained—never. In fact, in the twenty-seven years that I knew Billy, I never saw him have a bad day. I never noticed him complaining about anything. And I never heard him say anything negative about anyone—ever. On December 26, 2010, Billy preached what would be his final sermon at the church I pastor. He called his message "Struggle Well." He was honest about the fear, pain, fatigue, dread, and even doubt that accompany suffering. At the same time, he pointed us to the Word of God, saying, "The Word is your cure." When we submit ourselves to God, who promises to never leave or forsake us, we can let go of fear and dread. He told us that "there's no fear in death because the gospel is real."

"The more you dread tomorrow," he said, "the more you lose today. So when you wake up in the morning and start thinking about tomorrow, tell yourself, *I'm not going to do it. I'm going to make today a great day.*" As he was staring death in the face, Billy modeled courage, a positive attitude, and faith for us. Even his doctors and nurses were blown away by his faith and peace.

The final three months of his life on earth were memorable, to say the least. Billy said that they were the best weeks of his life. In January 2011, Billy had a near-death experience. We rushed him to the hospital and found out that he had blood clots lodging in his lungs. That night, Billy saw what he described as a set of stairs like those at a football stadium with a bright light at the end. Billy later said the Lord was giving him the opportunity to come to heaven right then if he wanted to. But Billy asked the Lord for a few more weeks so he could tell the people he cared for most how much he loved them and what they meant to him—and after about twenty-four hours, the light faded, the stairs disappeared, and Billy got better.

During the last eight weeks of Billy's life, he had over three hundred people, mostly out-of-town guests, visit him either in the hospital or at his house. Most came to pray for Billy and encourage him, but inevitably Billy would pray for and minister to them. I was there for most of these visits, and almost everyone who came hugged him and cried. Most of them said the same thing: "Thank you for believing in me." One such visitor was a pastor whom my father-in-law had helped after this man's first two attempts at church planting had failed. Everyone, including the denomination this pastor was a part of, had given up on him. Not Billy. Billy encouraged him and connected him with ARC, our church planting organization. This man's church now has thousands of members.

Billy finally went to be with Jesus on March 23, 2011. At the end of the day, he will not be known for what he did but for who he was. Billy loved God, and he loved people. He also made a choice to love life—food, fishing, hunting, music, and family—and he always made things fun. Every day was a great day.

LIFE OVERFLOWING

My father-in-law gave us a glimpse into what Jesus is like. It's clear that everyone—children, sinners, skeptics, the rich, the poor—loved being around Jesus. In fact, the only people who did not enjoy Jesus were the fake, inauthentic, self-righteous, religious people. Everyone else was drawn to Jesus because he was enjoyable to be around.

One reason people loved being around Jesus was that he gave the people around him breath, life, energy, peace, and joy. He came to restore our relationship with God and to put fresh air back in our lives. Some people don't believe this and define their faith, or more accurately, their religion, as a series of dos and don'ts. I believe Jesus had people living in such joy-draining environments in mind when he said, "The thief comes only in order to steal and kill and destroy.

I came that they may have and enjoy life, and have it in abundance (to the full, till it overflows)" (John 10:10, AMP).

People who have God's breath inside them seem to savor each day as a gift. Like my dear friend Billy, they enjoy life to the fullest. These people are winsome and attractive, which only draws others to them. They seem to relish each new day as one of promise and hope, opportunity and optimism. Their lives aren't any easier than anyone else's, and yet they rarely complain or dwell on their losses. They remember the past without remaining tied to it. They enjoy the present as a tremendous gift. They anticipate the future with great hope. They have influence and use it to positively encourage and shape those around them.

And yet from my experience, this is not how most of us live. Instead, we're pulled and pushed from one set of demands and expectations to another, from home to work to school to church, always reacting and trying to survive. There never seems to be time to be proactive and get *Savor each day as a gift.* ahead. But when we just go through the motions and try to keep up with everyone else, then we lose our joy. We end up back in the doldrums, going around in circles, eventually wondering why we're doing what we're doing.

Real life comes from God living inside us, and we are more likely to experience a breath of fresh air when our attitudes reflect the light of his presence. And attitudes can be adjusted. Most of us develop an outlook over time that becomes our default way of seeing things. Our thoughts shape our emotions, which affect our perceptions, which influence our actions. If we want to get the wind back in our sails, we must begin by examining the fundamental thoughts we carry around inside us. I'm convinced that there are some foundational beliefs that we can harness and use as a wind generator in our lives. Let's look at some of them now.

FIRST, APPRECIATE LIFE

If joy is supposed to be a sign of our Christian faith, then I'm afraid many of us are missing the mark. Most nonbelievers who watch us from a distance seem to view us the same way the movies portray Jesus—as long-faced, serious, pious, gloomy, out-of-touch people. But when we look at Scripture and consider the interactions Jesus had with those around him, we see that joy should indeed character-ize our faith.

Satan has the world fooled into thinking that sin is exciting and fun and that serving God is boring and tedious. Of course, it's just the opposite! Ask anybody who's ever experienced the throes of an addiction and they'll tell you that nothing is more deadening and draining than doing the same thing over and over again with no true benefits. Because of the law of diminishing returns, our sinful attempts at pleasure provide less and less satisfaction. We realize how empty we feel and how disappointed we are.

So let's set the record straight. When we have a relationship with God as our Father and completely rely on him, our lives will never be boring again. Just before going to the cross, Jesus explained to his disciples that they could experience the power and enjoy the love that existed between him and his heavenly Father. Then he said, "I have told you this so that my joy may be in you and that your joy may be complete" (John 15:11). Following the example of Jesus puts us on a grand adventure, one that will surprise and delight us much more than anything we could have ever dreamed up on our own.

We can't enjoy each day if we don't have a high appreciation for life. In order to cherish the life we've been given, we must never forget that God is working out his purposes for good. Even when we can't imagine it, even when times are hard and the pain feels unbearable, we must remember to exercise our faith and hope for God's best. Paul reflects this kind of attitude when he describes his outlook in the midst of multiple hardships as "sorrowful, yet always rejoicing; poor, yet making many rich; having nothing, and yet possessing everything" (2 Corinthians 6:10). No matter what happened, Paul didn't let circumstances upset his peace or shake his faith. This is the attitude that all of us can share when we place our trust in God. Though we may not yet understand how our situation will work out, we remain confident, knowing that God is taking care of it.

If you want to breathe new life into your attitude, then you must be able to laugh. If you can't tell already—and I sure hope you can—I love to laugh. "There is a time for everything and a season for every activity under heaven . . . a time to laugh" (Ecclesiastes 3:1, 4). Some people think it's inappropriate to laugh in church or irreverent to relate laughter with the sacredness of our faith in God. For them, church and religion are a serious business that requires the sobriety of a judge in a courtroom.

But I believe that God loves laughter, which reflects a sense of joy in our lives. We're told "A cheerful heart is good medicine" (Proverbs 17:22) and "the joy of the LORD is your strength" (Nehemiah 8:10). Jesus certainly displayed joy and humor. Consider how people were drawn to him. Parents even brought their children to be blessed by him. Unlike his disciples, who scolded the adults for bothering their teacher, Jesus welcomed the children. Imagine someone who likes to have kids around. Typically that person has a twinkle in his eye and a smile on his face.

The best day of your life is today, this one you're currently in. Accept the present as the gift God intends it to be and make the most of it. Don't squander it by worrying about the past or the future. Wake up and be in your life right at this moment.

PEOPLE WHO NEED PEOPLE

One of the best ways we experience our lives to the fullest is by loving people. Not just some people—everyone we encounter, even the ones we don't like. Billy, my father-in-law, invited people into his world. He would take them out to eat, out hunting, out fishing, and even on work projects. The closer he got to them and the closer he allowed them to get to him, the more they trusted, admired, and received from him. One of the life lessons I learned from watching Billy interact with others is that people can either irritate you or entertain you. They can either be considered a problem to be avoided or a person like you who just wants to be loved. As John Maxwell often says, people don't care how much you know until they know how much you care. Billy got that.

Many people point to other people as the reason they don't enjoy their lives. They've been wounded and disappointed so many times that they're skeptical, even cynical, about the motives of everyone they meet. They assume others are insincere and dishonest, unreliable and manipulative, just waiting to use or abuse them. So they stay defensive and on guard, either scaring people away with their harsh, unloving attitude, or else running away themselves. If this is the place where you find yourself, then it's time to be healed of your bitterness. Consider what the Bible says: "Let him who wants to enjoy life and see good days [good—whether apparent or not] keep his tongue free from evil and his lips from guile (treachery, deceit)" (1 Peter 3:10, AMP).

Our hearts become polluted with unresolved issues and old grudges when we allow someone else to get under our skin. Obviously, we didn't choose to be hurt, betrayed, or offended, but we always have a choice about how we react. And God makes it crystal clear how we must respond if we want to enjoy life: it's summed up by the word *forgiveness.*

If we don't forgive others, we're only hurting ourselves, not them. As the old adage reminds us, "Unforgiveness is like drinking poison and expecting someone else to die." Our unwillingness to forgive other people will keep us from experiencing and receiving the forgiveness our Father extends to us. If we're so obsessed with exacting revenge or getting an apology from someone who's hurt us, then we're missing the point of God's grace.

One of the many things I appreciate about Jesus is how he loved the unlovely. Here he was, pure holiness and perfection, God come to earth, and yet he was not afraid to embrace imperfect, flawed, impure people. His holiness didn't drive people away—just the opposite! They were attracted to the life, the hope, the breath of fresh air that he offered them. Jesus had dinner with tax collectors. He freed a woman who had been caught in adultery and was about to be stoned. He healed those who were weak and in need.

Based on Jesus' example, we must make a decision about how we're going to treat other people. He accepted them, loved them, believed in them. He never piled guilt on them or condemned them as the religious leaders seemed to enjoy doing. He always respected people, encouraged them, offered them hope where they had given up. We're called to extend the same kind of love to those around us. That includes the incompetent boss or passive-aggressive supervisor, the grumpy teacher and the inconsiderate neighbor, as well as the mean-spirited bully and the uptight attorney. Scripture makes it clear that we're called to put our faith in action: "Little children, let us stop just *saying* we love people; let us *really* love them, and *show it* by our *actions*" (1 John 3:18, TLB).

Of course, your love for others will find fuel in your love for God himself. As I shared earlier, my life message is to encourage people to draw closer to Jesus. That's because I know what it's like to move from a life-draining, exhausting, self-propelled faith to one that's life-giving, invigorating, and Spirit-propelled. Discover more of who God is. Enjoy the fullness of who he is as your Lord, your Father, your Creator. Look to him as your source of significance and satisfaction. How can you fall more deeply in love with your Savior? That is what the next chapters are all about.

BED ATTITUDE

Knowing how to adjust our attitudes can be easy; putting new practices in place can be another story. But we certainly didn't get the mind-set we presently have overnight. It developed over time and through many different experiences. Similarly, it takes time and an ongoing commitment to practice the habits that can transform our attitudes.

First, I believe we must make a conscious choice every day about how we want to respond to what happens that day. It's so easy to blame other people, to hold on to grudges from the past, to keep our emotions knotted around devastating pain from injurious events. But we have a choice about how we're going to live.

We can't determine what happens to us, but we can determine what happens in us.

We may not have had the same choices in the past, especially when we were growing up, but as adults we can choose how we will approach any challenges that come up. We can't determine what happens to us, but we can determine what happens in us. Paul makes the distinction very clear for us: "Let us throw off everything that hinders and the sin that so easily entangles. And let us run with perseverance the race marked out for us" (Hebrews 12:1).

I've found the best way to start off each day is by getting my mind-set right. Maybe you're familiar with one of my favorite prayers:

Dear Lord,
So far today, I'm doing all right. I haven't gossiped, lost my
temper, been greedy, grumpy, nasty, selfish, or self-indulgent.
I have not whined, cursed, or eaten too much chocolate.
However, I'm going to get out of bed in a few minutes, and
I will need a lot more help after that. Amen.

Seriously, when we begin each day by communicating with our Father, then we're going to feel a whole lot more connected to him. If we take the time to let him know how much we love him and to ask him for help, then we're making a choice about how our day will go. Here's an even better prayer to pray: "May these words of my mouth and this meditation of my heart be pleasing in your sight, LORD, my Rock and my Redeemer" (Psalm 19:14).

When we begin the day by giving God thanks and worshiping him, we've grounded ourselves in what is real, in what matters most. No matter what happens that day, we know that God is in charge and working out his sovereign plan for good. When we acknowledge and appreciate what we have, we're not as inclined to look for green grass over the fence. We know that God provides for us and wants to bless us with his abundant generosity.

Another of the most refreshing choices we can make each day is to forgive, which, as we mentioned earlier, is also an attitude. Jesus not only told us to forgive others, but to do it quickly and to practice it as many times as necessary. That's why he told Peter we should forgive "seventy times seven" times when his disciple asked how many times we should forgive someone. Jesus didn't want us to forgive others just to let them off the hook; he knew doing so would put wind back in our sails.

When we begin the day by worshiping and thanking God, we have grounded ourselves in what is real, in what matters most.

One of the great scientists of our country, George Washington Carver, stated, "I will never let another man ruin my life by making me hate him." As an African American pioneering his scientific discoveries in a racially prejudiced society, I'm sure Carver had due cause to hate people who treated him unfairly. But he knew that the only way to move forward is to forgive. He knew that he had a choice and decided he would never let someone else take that away from him, no matter what the offense.

Another hero of the faith to me was Billy's mom, a Cajun French woman named Williamette Plauche Hornsby. She was one of the sweetest souls you could ever hope to meet. Always in a good mood, always happy to see you, she was married to one of the hardest men you'd ever meet, my wife's grandfather. But his stubborn ways and hard-hearted decisions never seemed to affect Ma Maw Hornsby.

Anytime someone complained around her, she'd say, "Oh, pfff! Just forget about it. You've got the world by the tail." And she meant it. She had learned the art of letting go of the daily barbs and thorns that might come her way. There are many times now when I've been in a situation where I'm getting angry and, suddenly, I think of Ma Maw Hornsby. Thinking of her makes me smile because she was right—a forgiving attitude is liberating.

THIS IS GOOD

Maybe these principles and applications sound obvious or trite to you, but I assure you that if you truly want to live life to the fullest, to have real joy and peace and purpose and satisfaction, then you have to avoid dismissing them as clichés or things you've heard before. You have to find a way to make these truths your own, to have them sink into your bones and become a part of who you really are. If you're still not sure how to do this, keep reading. You'll learn how to do this later in the book.

When you do begin to adjust your attitude and experience fresh wind in your sails, then you will discover a renewed appreciation for life. You won't take the hard times so seriously or so personally. You'll realize that each day is all you have. You'll love others and let them know it. You'll laugh at yourself and at the strange, wonderful, crazy things that happen in your life.

And sometimes, usually in hindsight, you'll see God's hand in places where you couldn't before—protecting you, guarding you, guiding you in ways that seemed hard at the time. In 1999, when I was stuck in the doldrums, I sought God because I was desperate to get rid of my depression. Yet all the while God was preparing to move me to Birmingham to plant a church. I just couldn't see it then.

People who have a high appreciation of life know that God is going to work everything out for the good. They may not always see it in this life, but they know they serve a good God who loves his children. They don't sweat the small stuff. They let their Father take care of it all. "And we know that in all things God works for the good of those who love him, who have been called according to his purpose" (Romans 8:28).

ARE YOU POSITIVE?

One of the simplest ways to adjust your attitude is to look for something positive in every situation. I'm not talking about becoming a Pollyanna who spiritualizes everything and pulls silver linings out of every storm cloud. But I am talking about being willing to see what you have in the midst of the storm.

Think about the people you know who complain about everything. They say things like, "This is it—I will never trust another living person again." My response to them: Really? Then you're in for a sad, sad life. Or, "This is the worst thing that's ever happened to me—I'll never get over this." Are you sure? Most people experience pain in this life and manage to push through and keep going. Or, "I really blew it this time!" Guess what? You'll probably blow it again. It's part of being human. But because you're human, you're able to fall down and get back on your feet again. God designed us to be amazingly resilient.

Whether it's rainy or sunny, stormy or calm, resilient people see the upside to their present position. They never lose sight of all they have to be grateful for because they've learned what Paul himself learned and passed on: "Give thanks in all circumstances; for this is God's will for you in Christ Jesus" (1 Thessalonians 5:18).

One of the most grateful people I've ever known was my

grandmother, my dad's mom. We called her Ma Maw Hodges, and she lived to be ninety-four years old. She lived a hard life, but you would never know it judging by her attitude. She was orphaned at age thirteen when her mother burned to death while boiling their clothes to avoid diphtheria. Ma Maw Hodges grew up and married the man who was my dad's father. And then the unbelievable happened: her husband was killed in a car wreck, leaving her with a one-year-old son (my dad) to raise.

Undaunted, she worked two jobs and brought up her son to be positive and hardworking, not a bitter victim of circumstance. Eventually, she married again, and her son took his stepfather's name. So I'm not really a Hodges by blood; my biological grandfather's name was Hampton. As she grew older, my grandmother suffered with crippling arthritis for many years. But I never heard her complain—not once.

Whenever anyone asked her how she was doing, Ma Maw Hodges's answer was always the same: "I'm better off than most." Her attitude was inspiring—like a breath of fresh air. Many times throughout her life, she chose to be happy. She knew the meaning of one of her favorite verses: "Whatever is true, whatever is noble, whatever is right, whatever is pure, whatever is lovely, whatever is admirable—if anything is excellent or praiseworthy—think about such things" (Philippians 4:8).

A NEW ATTITUDE

Finally, if we want to experience fresh air in our attitudes, we must turn all of our worries over to God. One of the primary reasons we're not happy is that we try to handle everything ourselves. Yet no one can handle everything—or even most things—in their lives. No matter how much money we have, no matter how advanced our technology becomes, humans will always be limited. In many ways, we basically make the same mistake that Adam and Eve made in the Garden, which is choosing to think we can be like God, over and over again.

The difficulties we face can't be our problem and God's problem at the same time. When we realize that he's in control, that he alone is God and is infinite, powerful, loving, and all-knowing, then it's suddenly much easier to relax and enjoy the present moment. He never intended for us to worry about what might happen, what could happen, what should happen, or what will happen. He only asks that we follow him and live in this moment right now.

We're told, "Do not be anxious about anything, but in every situation, by prayer and petition, with thanksgiving, present your requests to God. And the peace of God, which transcends all understanding, will guard your hearts and your minds in Christ Jesus" (Philippians 4:6-7).

> *The difficulties we face can't be our problem and God's problem at the same time. When we realize that he's in control, it's much easier to relax and enjoy the present moment.*

Notice that prayer and thanksgiving are gifts God offers us so that we may access his peace. We can also rest and be refreshed in his presence as we read Scripture, pray, worship, and serve others, some of the practices we'll look at in the coming chapters.

God wants us to rely on him. "Cast all your anxiety on him because he cares for you" (1 Peter 5:7). When we give him our concerns, we naturally have an attitude that's worry free, that's at peace, that's present to love those around us.

Like my father-in-law or the wonderful grandmothers in our family, we can be a force for good in this life. We can display the heart of Christ in everything we do, showing others who God really is. We can be content and compassionate, relaxed and resilient.

BREATHING LESSON

On the day Billy died, I promised the Lord that I would do everything I could to live my life the way Billy did. Attitude is a choice. And for most of us, our attitude will not take care of itself. We need to manage it every day. One of the healthiest things you can do is take responsibility for your own attitude. The key is to focus on what happens *in* you, not *to* you. The choice is yours.

By spending time watching people like Billy and Ma Maw Hodges who attracted people to them by their joy, good humor, and love, I learned to begin adopting a similar outlook. Who has modeled the character of Jesus for you in your life? How have they influenced you to grow closer to God and be a life-giver? I encourage you to let their example be an inspiration and model for you to follow so you'll become a breath of fresh air to others like they are for you.

Let the Spirit renew your thoughts and attitudes. . . .
Imitate God, therefore, in everything you do, because
you are his dear children. Live a life filled with love,
following the example of Christ.

EPHESIANS 4:23; 5:1-2, NLT

CHAPTER 6

THE BOOK IS ALIVE

·····································

To what greater inspiration and counsel can we turn than to the
imperishable truth to be found in this treasure house, the Bible?

QUEEN ELIZABETH II

When my wife and I first got married, we lived in a little eight-hundred-square-foot town house in Baton Rouge. It qualified as a town house simply because it had an upstairs with a tiny bedroom, but not much more. We didn't mind the close quarters, though. Like most newlyweds, we were happy just to be together.

One morning, after we'd been there about a year, Tammy and I came downstairs and couldn't believe our eyes. The entire first floor of our little home had been stripped bare! You know how the homes in Whoville looked after the Grinch came and took everything? Well, he must have paid us a visit because it was cleaner than when we'd moved in. Both the front door and back door, only about ten feet apart, were swinging wide open.

We ran outside to the little parking lot of our complex, and sure enough, both our cars parked in front had also been broken into. We were speechless and just looked at each other with disbelief through tearful eyes. How were we able to sleep through such a huge theft? Our stereo, TV, VCR, kitchen appliances, even our cars' cassette players—stolen and never to be seen by us again. If you've ever been violated by a crime like this, then you know that you lose more than just your possessions. You lose your peace of mind. Your sense of security and your ability to relax go out the door with your property. You have trouble sleeping because the thieves know where you live and know how to get into your home. You're scared and paranoid about being robbed again. You can't help it. You try to be tough, but inside you're terrified of it happening again and feel powerless to do anything about it.

In the days that followed, my wife and I prayed, met with the police, talked with friends, family, and each other, and did everything we could to turn our loss over to God and move on with our lives. Nothing seemed to work until the day we found this passage in the Psalms: "There will be no breaching of walls, no going into captivity, no cry of distress in our streets. Blessed are the people of whom this is true; blessed are the people whose God is the LORD" (144:14-15).

The words felt tailor-made for us and our situation. God was still larger and more powerful than any thief, any robber, any thug who violated our home and stole our property. God would deal with them on his terms, so we didn't have to worry about it. And we didn't have to be afraid any longer; God would always be our protection and refuge.

Tammy and I printed that passage on a couple of index cards and stuck one on the front door and the other on the back door. We posted God's Word as a guard around our house. It wasn't like a magic barrier or anything like that, although as we'll discuss in a moment, the Scriptures definitely contain God's power and authority. No, we posted those verses to remind us of what was true, that God was with us no matter what. Every time we saw one of those cards, our confidence grew and our fear subsided.

DAILY CHORES

As you think about my story, keep in mind what I've already told you about my early life as a Christian: I was in the doldrums. This included a flat prayer life and an indifference about the Word of God. I certainly respected it as divine and inerrant and knew I was supposed to study it and learn about God and his character. I knew it was the ultimate handbook for how to live a purpose-driven, fulfilled life as a follower of Jesus. And yet, it seemed like pure drudgery to read my Bible on a daily basis, a chore that had to be done just so I could say I did it and get on with my day.

It was like making the bed or doing the dishes. You couldn't just do it once and then let it go for months and months. If you were a good Christian, then you did it every day, or at least several times a week. But that didn't mean it would be enjoyable or even relevant to what was going on in your life. It was just a good practice to remind yourself and others that you took your faith seriously.

Can you relate to my experience? How would you describe your relationship with your Bible right now? Do you feel a twinge of guilt when the topic comes up because you feel like you should read it more often? Or do you feel a sense of satisfaction because you read yours this morning? Let me challenge you: think not only about the last time you read your Bible but what you read. What stuck with you?

Not much had been sticking with me. After the break-in, though, and in other times of need, I began to see the Bible differently. I had a new appreciation for how the Bible applied to my everyday life. And as my sails filled with the breath of God, and my passion and excitement for my faith expanded, I began to realize that I had to rethink my view of the Bible. I didn't want to take it for granted or approach reading it as a chore.

Imagine coming home to discover that your spouse has sent the kids to their grandparents and a special dinner for two awaits you. There's candlelight and soft music playing, and your spouse has dressed in your favorite outfit. Would you respond by saying, "Again? Do we have to have another romantic dinner and kiss and stuff? Okay, whatever . . ." That would be pretty insulting, wouldn't it? I wonder if God feels that way when we regard his Word so dispassionately.

The Bible is obviously indispensable to the Christian faith; if you attempt to follow Jesus without it, you're not going to get very far. But the Bible is much more than an ancient manual full of historical stories and dos and don'ts. It's a divine wind machine, inflating our sails with God's breath, giving us direction and purpose, and propelling us forward. Jesus said, "The Spirit gives life; the flesh counts for nothing. The *words* I have spoken to you are spirit [breath] and they are life" (John 6:63, emphasis mine. In the original Greek language, which the New Testament was written in, the word *spirit* literally means "breath.")

> *The Bible is a divine wind machine, inflating our sails with God's breath, giving us direction and purpose, and propelling us forward.*

Jesus is telling us that his words, the messages that he came to deliver, are not normal words. Basically he's saying, "These words I've spoken to you are breath, a blast of wind to give you life." Or put another way, "My words are fresh air for you."

POWER WORDS

The entire Bible has this kind of strength, as I see it. God's Word has the power to bring about its own fulfillment. It's alive and dynamic and meets you where you are if you let it sink into your heart and mind. Like a compass that's always at true North, it can dramatically alter your life's course and show you who God is and who you are. It can transform the way you live and help you discern what's from God and what's not. In fact, it tells us what it can do: "The word of God is living and active. Sharper than any double-edged sword, it penetrates even to dividing soul and spirit, joints and marrow; it judges the thoughts and attitudes of the heart" (Hebrews 4:12). God's Word is alive, and if you'll let it, it will cut through anything you face. So don't just read the Bible; let the Bible read you.

As you do, the Bible will align your emotions and mind with God as you make day-to-day decisions. There's nothing too difficult, too painful, too embarrassing, too human, or too earthy for it to address. The people populating its pages can inspire you, coach you, challenge you, instruct you, and sometimes amaze you if you'll let them.

So how do you and I get there? How can we reach the point where reading the Bible engages us and brings us joy and helps us interact with God? Like dough that needs an ingredient to make it rise, the Bible requires our faith in order to be activated in our lives. Faith serves as the catalyst that enables us to take the necessary steps of obedience as we follow God and listen to his Word.

Why did the Israelites have to wander around the desert for forty years rather than march right into the land God had promised them? According to the New Testament, they heard God's words but didn't trust him to fulfill what he had promised. "We also have had the gospel preached to us, just as they did; but the message they heard was of no value to them, because those who heard did not combine it with faith" (Hebrews 4:2).

Reading the Word only out of a sense of duty is like trying to make dynamite without nitroglycerin. It simply won't ignite. When we don't have faith, or we don't bring it to our encounter with the Word, then we view it in a flat, lifeless way that many would say feels "boring."

Has that been your experience? Maybe you've read the Bible and it was of no value because you just didn't get it. Or you went to church and listened to a message and it was like hearing someone lecture in a foreign language because it just didn't seem to make much sense. According to this verse from Hebrews, when you lack faith as you read God's Word, its truth can't take root in your heart and life.

Okay, Chris, you may be thinking, *you're telling me that I don't have enough faith for the Bible to come alive. So what am I supposed to do about it? I'm not sure I can just flip a switch and make all this God stuff work.* I hear you. Or maybe you're thinking, *I've had times when the Scriptures seemed alive and relevant to me, but I seem to have lost it. How much faith do I need to get back to that place?* Another fair question.

In fact, if you think you have to conjure up faith on your own, you'll always be frustrated. The key ingredient in making faith work is God's revelation. Let me explain. Have you ever tried to solve a problem for a while when suddenly the solution seemed crystal clear and you wanted to shout, "Eureka!"? God's revelation is the "aha!" moment when you connect the dots and realize not only what the real problem is, but how it pertains to your life and what to do about it. Every time a passage from the Bible makes you think, *Now I understand; now the Bible has totally come alive to me*, your faith is activated.

> *Every time a passage from the Bible makes you think,* Now I understand; now the Bible has totally come alive to me, *your faith is activated.*

Curiously enough, in Greek, the language used for the original manuscripts of the New Testament, there are two different terms for the word "word." One is used to describe the kind of insight and illumination we've been talking about, an epiphany where all the lights come on. This word is *rhema*, and it is distinct from the Greek word for "word," *logos*, which refers to the literal words on the page as you're reading them now. *Rhema* is more than just the words themselves; it's the process of understanding them, of having eyes to see and ears to hear. It's almost like reading between the lines so that you get a sense of the real message and its relevance and application to your life.

THE AHA! MOMENT

So many of us get stuck focusing just on the *logos* (the written word) that we don't press into having a deeper encounter with the *rhema* (the revealed word). Remember that you're going to need faith if God's Word is going to come alive for you, and in order to have your faith activated, you need to experience revelation. Let me give you one of the best examples of this kind of revelation I can think of.

You've probably heard how the angel Gabriel visited a teenage girl named Mary to let her know she would become pregnant with a child who would be the Messiah her people longed for.

Some scholars say that Mary was between thirteen and sixteen years old. If you have kids, especially teenagers, this fact may blow your mind. Here's this young lady, minding her own business, when an angel drops in to tell her, "God finds favor with you and has an assignment for you if you're willing to do it. You're going to be the mother of his baby, okay?"

Mary responds like most of us would: "How can this be? I'm still a virgin." At this point, the communication between the two of them is at the *logos* level. The angel is saying something that is entirely true, and yet Mary can't comprehend his message because it doesn't make sense logically. It defies what she knows about human reproduction.

Here's where the "aha!" moment kicks in. The angel explains, "Here's how it's going to happen. The Holy Spirit, the wind and the breath of God, is going to enter you, and he is actually going to overshadow you so that this child will be conceived immaculately." Then the angel Gabriel adds the key phrase: "*Nothing* is impossible with God" (Luke 1:37, emphasis added).

Now, this may sound like a great motivational bumper sticker to us, but it's so much more. In the Greek, the expression for "nothing" is actually two words, "no word [*rhema*]." So let me put it together for you with this in mind. Basically the angel tells Mary, "I know you may not get it now, but if what I'm saying ever becomes a revelation to you, then nothing is impossible." Or here's my translation: No word that God speaks, when it becomes a revelation to you, will lack the power for its fulfillment. There's nothing in the Bible that, when it becomes an "oh, now I get it!" moment, lacks the power to actually happen inside you.

Mary gets it. She tells the angel, "I am the Lord's servant. May it be to me as you have said" (Luke 1:38). How does she get it? And better yet, how do we get it?

Let's review for a moment:

1. Faith activates the Word. How do you grow your faith?
2. Revelation activates faith. And how do you get a revelation?
3. Meditation on Scripture activates, or is the means to, revelation. We'll talk about this one next.

CHEW YOUR FOOD

Throughout the Old and New Testaments, we're told numerous times in numerous ways to meditate on God's Word. The Old Testament was originally written in Hebrew, and one of the meanings for the Hebrew word for *meditate* is "rumination," the same word used to describe a cow chewing its cud. (In fact, the process of rechewing the cud to further break down plant matter and stimulate digestion is called ruminating.) I'm guessing you haven't driven by a field lately and said, "Hey, look at that cow over there meditating!"

Now, if you don't have a farming background, you may be wondering what in the world it means for a cow to ruminate or chew its cud—and what's a cud, anyway? As gross as it sounds, "cud" is the food a cow ingests, chews, swallows, regurgitates, and then chews some more before swallowing again. According to animal scientists, cows spend about eight hours a day chewing their cud, which works out to about thirty thousand chews. Because of the way their digestive systems are configured, it's critical that cows keep chewing over and over again to moisten their food and break it down into smaller pieces.[5]

Similarly, we should meditate on God's Word in such a way that it stays with us. We're so bombarded with information each day—e-mails, Facebook messages, tweets, reports, articles, letters, notes, magazines, and books. It's gotten to the point that most of us don't read anymore; we skim. We usually comprehend only what we need in the moment, whether to respond to an e-mail or to write the report for work, and then go on to the next task. Rarely do we read something and think about it and ponder it and think about it some more and then go back and read it again and again.

But we're told, "Do not let this Book of the Law depart from your *mouth*; *meditate* on it. . . ." Chew it, swallow it, regurgitate it, and chew it some more so you can get all the flavor out. And when should we be doing this? ". . . day and night, so that you may be careful to do everything written in it. *Then* you will be prosperous and successful" (Joshua 1:8, emphasis mine).

I want what's after *then* ("prosperous and successful") but need to do what's before *then* ("meditate"). Perhaps you can relate. Simply put, if we want the Bible to be revealed, then we need to commit to meditating on it.

THE LAST WORD

In order to experience the breath of life that comes from reading the Bible, and in order for Scripture to come alive and remain dynamic in all areas of our lives, we need to focus on three key principles.[6]

First, we must accept the authority of Scripture. Unfortunately, we live in a culture that seems to intentionally attack the authority and validity of God's Word. Rather than allowing the Word to change them, many people seem to want to change the Bible to fit their preferences. Hollywood has done it, the news media often does it, and, I'm afraid, even the church has done it sometimes. A recent study found that only

> *If you want the Bible to be revealed, then you need to commit to meditating on it.*

9 percent of American adults have a biblical worldview, which is predicated on the belief that the Bible is completely accurate in all the principles it teaches.[7]

Although I realize I may be outnumbered, I boldly proclaim that I'm in that 9 percent minority who believes that the Bible is alive, perfect, totally relevant, totally true, righteous, holy, and from God. The Word of God is timeless and transcends cultures and nationalities and denominations. It has the final say on all aspects of our lives. It truly has the last word.

When we accept the authority of the Bible, we commit to reading it and then taking what it says as the ultimate source of truth. That is the approach the apostle Paul commends in 1 Thessalonians 2:13: "We never stop thanking God that when you received his message from us, you didn't think of our words as mere human ideas. You accepted what we said as the very word of God—which, of course, it is. And this word continues to work in you who believe" (NLT).

The psalmist tells us that blessed are those who "delight in the law of the LORD, meditating on it day and night" (Psalm 1:2, NLT). They don't "join in with mockers" who scorn God and his Word (verse 1). He goes on to say that people who respect God's Word are like trees firmly planted by a stream of water, whose leaves never wither. Whatever they set their hands to will prosper.

> *When you give the Bible the authority it deserves, it will speak into your life with clarity and certainty.*

When you're in doubt or uncertain, when you're confused or frustrated, turn to Scripture. "All Scripture is God-breathed and is useful for teaching, rebuking, correcting and training in righteousness" (2 Timothy 3:16). When you give the Bible the authority it deserves, then it will speak into your life with clarity and certainty. You will go from reading words on the page—*logos*—to having ongoing "aha!" moments, or *rhema*.

DAILY DIET

Next, we must make our relationship with the Bible part of our everyday lives. We are to be in the Word every day, not out of duty or to feel better about ourselves, but because doing so gives us room to meditate, which is the pathway to revelation and faith. The Bible is not a once-a-week, Sunday kind of book. It's not even a morning devotional book, but instead it's like food, something you and I need every day. Something to be devoured and digested, chewed on and chewed some more.

Too often, we allow someone to serve us a tiny Bible morsel on a platter once a week and then we wonder why we're weak, stuck in one place, or lost in the doldrums. Now I don't know about you, but I don't eat three meals a day. I eat about five times a day. I get up in the morning and eat something. That usually holds me until lunch. When I get hungry again around 3 or 4 in the afternoon, I have a snack. Then there's dinner around 6 and usually another snack before bedtime. Yep, I pretty much eat all day long!

One of my favorite practices of daily Bible reading is using the *One Year Bible*. This daily reading plan consists of passages from the Old Testament, New Testament, Psalms, and Proverbs. Each day's reading takes only about fifteen minutes. At year's end, I have read through the whole Bible. I start each day this way and try to find just one verse from all the readings for that day that I can chew on all day long, returning to get more bites throughout the day. I may even try to memorize a verse or print it on a little card to carry around with me all day long.

Sometimes the verse I choose to meditate on comes not from my daily reading, but from a concern I have that I need to turn over to the Lord. I opened this chapter by telling you how the passage from Psalms comforted and restored Tammy and me after the burglary in our home. When our kids started driving, I paraphrased Psalm 121:8 and kept it in front of me: "God is going to bless our coming and going both now and forevermore." I'm not sure who needed the blessing more in this case, me for my nerves or my kids for their driving! Surely God knows how much better they drive than I do!

Are you afraid and finding yourself awake at night worrying? Try Psalm 27:1: "The LORD is my light and my salvation, whom shall I fear?" Do you have money issues going on? Then you had better know Philippians 4:19: "My God will meet all your needs according to the riches of his glory in Christ Jesus." There's even a verse for going to the dentist—"Crown him with many crowns!" Just kidding—that's not a verse. But there is a verse that says, "Open wide your mouth and I will fill it" (Psalm 81:10).

The third and final thing to remember is quite simple: just do it. Accept the Bible's authority, make it an ongoing part of your everyday life, and then put it into practice. Live it, do it, practice it. When God's Word says to love, put it into practice. When it says to give, give. James tells us, "Don't just listen to God's word. You must do what it says. Otherwise, you are only fooling yourselves" (James 1:22, NLT).

Our goal should be to take the living Word and plant it into the world around us. Into our relationships and our work. Into our classrooms and our cubicles. Into our kitchens and our bedrooms. Into our bank accounts and our bill paying. *Everywhere.*

BREATHING LESSON

The Bible is not a normal book. Its contents aren't just text on a page. Those words contain the supernatural power to attain their own fulfillment. The Bible has breath in it, the God-essence that makes all the difference in the world. If you want to experience transformation in your life, if you want to live a vibrant adventure instead of spin circles in the doldrums, read your Bible and notice how it propels you forward.

It's up to you to take the next step. Read the Bible every day because it is alive and the only Book that ultimately matters. Then just live it.

> In the beginning was the Word, and the Word was with God, and the Word was God. He was with God in the beginning. Through him all things were made; without him nothing was made that has been made. In him was life, and that life was the light of all mankind. The light shines in the darkness, and the darkness has not overcome it.
>
> JOHN 1:1-5

CHAPTER 7

ENJOYING PRAYER

....

To be a Christian without prayer is no more possible
than to be alive without breathing.
MARTIN LUTHER KING JR.

As a teenager in the church where I grew up, I was the youngest guy the pastor would call on to pray. The first time it happened, I was probably eleven or twelve. It was a summer Sunday night service, and there weren't many people there. I think Brother Dean figured that it wouldn't matter much if I messed up, since not that many members would hear me. At the end of the service, after we'd had an altar call (yes, even on Sunday nights—people need Jesus all the time, right?), he would usually call on one of the men of the church to pray—some sturdy pillar who had been there for decades and had a dozen eloquent prayers memorized for any occasion.

But that summer evening, as the last light of the sun painted the sky with scarlet streaks, Brother Dean called on me. "It was good to see everyone here tonight. Now, Chris, would you be willing to close us in prayer?" It was one of those surreal moments when time stood still. Like in *The Matrix* when a bullet is flying in slow motion, it seemed like hours passed between the sound of his words and the realization in my head that he was talking to me.

You see, I had been weighing in my mind whether or not my parents would let me go to Dairy Queen with some other kids after church. Talk about switching gears—from imagining the taste of a hot fudge sundae to delivering a benediction in a matter of seconds! I looked around, but there were no other people named Chris in our church that night. Just me. Every pair of eyes in the sanctuary seemed to be staring at me. I looked over at my dad, and he was sort of smiling, giving me an encouraging look, as if to say, "Go on. You can do it!"

So I stood up, cleared my throat, closed my eyes, and started, "Uh, th-thank you, Lord, for this message tonight. We ask . . . that your message would remain in our hearts and go with us . . . through this week. Thank you for the gift . . . of your most precious gift, er, Son . . . and thank you for the message Brother Dean gave us tonight." Deep breath—how many times can you repeat the word *message*? Then I set a new speed record for uttering one sentence: "We ask all of this through the name of your Son, our Savior, Jesus Christ. Amen."

Brother Dean smiled and said, "And all God's people said? Amen. Thank you, Chris; mighty fine." My face was flushed red with embarrassment. I was still reeling from the shock that he had even asked me. I'm not sure why he picked me—maybe because my father played the organ and our family was there every time the doors opened. Maybe because I was pretty outgoing and was used to speaking to adults with respect and courtesy like any good Southern boy should. Maybe because he hoped that someday I would actually be excited enough about my relationship with God to enjoy praying.

PRAY LIKE YOU MEAN IT

As much as we might think otherwise, *enjoying prayer* is not an oxymoron, like jumbo shrimp or icy hot. From my experience, both personally and as a pastor, if there's one area where people find the least amount of enjoyment, it's with prayer. We all know we need to do it, but few Christians have been able to discover how to enjoy taking the time to talk to God.

If, like me, you were raised in the church, then there's a good chance that prayer became something detached from the rest of your faith—something lifeless, boring, stagnant. It was a speech to be endured, like a teacher's lecture, or words that you knew were important but that seemed to run together, like the fire marshal's code. As I've studied prayer in the Bible, I've discovered that most people today pray very differently from what's described in Scripture. There's not one place where it says that when you pray you should close your eyes. And there's certainly not one place where it tells you to speak in a soft, quiet, reverent monotone, addressing God as if he were from England. (I think some people assume it must be more official if you pray like the King James Version—"thou knowest of what I speaketh.") Imagine addressing your spouse and kids as if you'd just stepped out of one of Shakespeare's plays!

Also, prayer can feel like drudgery if you worry too much about how long you pray. I remember once as a teenager hearing a sermon on Jesus and his disciples in the garden of Gethsemane. The preacher told us that Jesus got after his disciples because they couldn't watch with him for an hour. Likewise, we were told, if we spent anything less than an hour in prayer, we weren't pleasing God either. I went home that day utterly discouraged. I had finally managed to pray fifteen minutes at a stretch, and now I had been told my prayer life was an utter failure.

Prayer is not nearly that complicated. Honestly, you are simply talking with someone you know and love. I'm a little embarrassed to share something so personal, but when I wake up in the morning, I tell God, "Good morning, Lord. It's good to see you. I've missed you. I'm glad we get to spend a few minutes together right now. I'm so grateful for how much you love me. You're my daddy, my Abba Father, and I love you today with all my heart."

If that sounds like something a child might pray, then I'm glad. That's how I want to approach God, as a son who's excited to love and serve his Father. When you pray, it really is just a conversation between you and the One who loves you most. Prayer can be one of the most dynamic, life-giving, breath-of-fresh-air places in your entire life.

Jesus certainly prayed a lot. In fact, all Jewish people learned how to pray when they were very young. They not only knew how to pray, but they had memorized prayers and knew when to use them and for which occasions. It was not only part of the religious practice but was also an expectation of cultural custom. Keeping this in mind, it's all the more interesting to read that Jesus' disciples asked him to teach them to pray. "One day Jesus was praying in a certain place. When he finished, one of his disciples said to him, 'Lord, teach us to pray'" (Luke 11:1).

PRAYER 101

Now here's my theory about this rather unique request: Since these Jewish disciples already knew how to pray based on their cultural upbringing, I don't think they were asking Jesus to teach them *how* to pray. Instead, I believe they were saying, "We don't know how to pray like you do—to receive that life-giving, breath-of-fresh-air experience that comes not from just saying a memorized prayer, but from being in conversation with God. When we pray, it doesn't look like that, not at all. Can you teach us to pray with passion, like we mean it?"

Jesus' response, of course, is the best-known prayer in the world, the Lord's Prayer. He said to his disciples, "Okay, I can teach you. After this manner, pray this. . . ." I believe Jesus then did what all the rabbis have done down through the ages when instructing their students in any area: he taught his followers the *topics* of prayer that they should bring before God. However, two thousand years later, we have turned the instructions into a prayer in and of itself. In my humble opinion, the Lord's Prayer was never intended by Jesus to be prayed verbatim just as he spoke it. It's okay if we do, but there's so much more to it than that.

When we recite the Lord's Prayer, or any prayer, from memory over and over again, there's always the danger that we're not considering exactly what we're saying. While I certainly seem to have topics and themes that come up a lot when I talk to my wife and kids ("Okay, there goes Dad again . . ."), I don't have a paragraph that I repeat word for word every time we talk.

The Lord's Prayer is an outline for our communication with God.

I'm not criticizing anyone for praying the Lord's Prayer as it appears in Scripture, only noting that the words themselves are not as important as the topics Jesus is covering in his model prayer. Basically, what he gives to his disciples, including us, is an outline for our communication with God.

Our Father which art in heaven, Hallowed be thy name. Thy kingdom come, Thy will be done in earth, as it is in heaven. Give us this day our daily bread. And forgive us our debts, as we forgive our debtors. And lead us not into temptation, but deliver us from evil: For thine is the kingdom, and the power, and the glory, for ever. Amen.

MATTHEW 6:9-13, KJV

Jesus' prayer outline has seven items based on the seven phrases that he uses. Let's look at them together and see how they can breathe fresh air into the way we talk to our Father.

TAKE IT PERSONALLY

Notice how Jesus begins his instruction on prayer. The first thing he teaches us to do is connect with God relationally: *our Father* who is in heaven. It's so important when we enter into our prayer time that we do as Jesus does and begin by calling God something that's endearing. So often we treat him like some distant, impersonal machine: "Oh, great and mighty God, we give Thee thanks . . . "

Jesus says, "No, no, no! You want to know my secret? Here's what you do. You begin with the assurance that God is your Father and loves you like a daddy loves his children. He wants to be in this relationship with you, not just as your God but as your Father."

Now addressing God as our dad may be a hurdle for some of us who had less-than-honorable earthly fathers. Many of us struggle to relate to God so intimately, and the word *father* may even conjure up negative images because of the baggage we have with our own dads. We're more comfortable keeping God at arm's length. So much about our relationship with God depends on how accurately we see him.

If we view him as the loving daddy he is, with his arms open wide, waiting to hold us, then we're going to enjoy spending time with him in conversation. However, if we view him as a faceless, angry giant with a club in his hand waiting to pounce on us, then it's no wonder we try to avoid him.

I used to struggle with how I viewed God. My view of him was based on an evangelism tract that depicted God as a cartoonlike king sitting on a big throne, the kind of chair that the statue of Honest Abe sits in at the Lincoln Memorial. In the tract, God had no discernible features, just a glowing light all around him. The cartoon people, by comparison, looked like little ants beside his feet. Another image I had of God came from one of my favorite movies growing up, *The Wizard of Oz*. God was just like the Mighty Oz—a big, scowling, green face enveloped in smoke, with a booming voice that told us to go do spiritual things: PRAY! PERFORM FOR ME!

Obviously, there was nothing positive about my mental image of God. Even as I got older and knew that God wasn't like my imagined version of him, I still struggled to know how to relate to him. That began to change as I studied the Bible and saw how close Jesus was to his Dad. Jesus brought us the freedom to relate to God in this same way. Paul wrote, "Those who are led by the Spirit of God are the children of God. The Spirit you received does not make you slaves, so that you live in fear again; rather, the Spirit you received brought about your adoption to sonship. And by him we cry, 'Abba, Father'" (Romans 8:14-15). The Greek word for "Spirit" here is *pneuma*, meaning God's breath of fresh air. Consider my translation based on this notion: God wants to put breath back in our sails through the fresh air of his Spirit because he's adopted us as his children.

So now we don't have to tremble like the Cowardly Lion before the Mighty Oz. We can run to our heavenly Father the way our own children run to greet us when we come home. The Aramaic word Paul uses here, *Abba*, is usually rendered as "Daddy," but it's warmer than that, more familiar. It's like "Papa! I'm so glad to see you" all rolled into one word. When I came to this realization about how we can relate to him, my old image of God went up in smoke. He is someone who wants to be with me and spend time with me.

NAME TAGS

Once we've established our relationship with God, Jesus tells us to honor our Father's name—"Hallowed be thy name." God's names, and he has many, each expressing a different facet of his magnificent being, have incredible power. According to Proverbs 18:10, his names are places of protection; the righteous can run there and be safe.

In this part of the Lord's Prayer, I picture Jesus telling us, "Look, the next thing to consider after you establish your personal relationship, your greeting, is the benefit you have in honoring God's names." We call him our Righteousness and remember that he has made us righteous. We're reminded that we don't have to depend on our own efforts anymore by making animal sacrifices and following the old letter of the Law.

As you may be aware, there are many names for God throughout the Scriptures: he is our Peace, our Protector, our Provider, and the list goes on and on. Each name carries with it a reminder of the distinct benefits we have in that aspect of God's relationship with us. We call out to him and we remember that he is a God who provides, a God who gives shelter, comfort, and the peace that passes understanding.

Next, Jesus lets us in on the real secret to our relationship with God—the key to how we talk to him. "Thy kingdom come, Thy will be done in earth, as it is in heaven." In other words, we need to pray and seek God's agenda first. Isn't it true that so often when we pray, we've got our laundry list of things to ask him for? But Jesus reminds us to first focus on what he wants done. When we follow his way of doing things and allow him to guide us, then he takes care of us by listening to our needs, "our daily bread" (more on this in a minute).

Have you ever noticed how much easier it is to relate to someone when you're willing to participate in their agenda before asking something of them? Recently, after a big storm, I had some major yard work that needed to be done, so I enlisted my sons. We were out lifting tree limbs, mowing and raking grass, and picking up rocks and sticks. My guys had the best attitude—they were doing a great job and doing it gladly. Well, all except my youngest, Joseph, who definitely didn't have yard work on his agenda for the day. At one point, he walked by me with a little stick and said, "You can thank me later."

When we finished several hours later, I wanted to do something special for my hardworking guys, so I grilled some burgers and we had a great dinner. As we were sitting around afterward, my middle son, David, said, "Hey, Dad—are you thinking it's a Krispy Kreme kind of night?" My immediate thought was, *Definitely! How many do you want?* because I remembered what a great job they'd done and their great attitudes. Since they had gladly participated in what I needed them to do, I was happy to do what they wanted in return.

It is so easy for all of us to become nearsighted and focus our prayers only on ourselves. "Thy kingdom come, Thy will be done" keeps us farsighted—attentive to God's agenda first. And if we want to know what our Father's primary agenda is, I don't think we have to look far. Foremost, he clearly wants to rescue those who are estranged from him, the lost sheep who've wandered off, the prodigals and the prostitutes, the tax collectors and the weak. Over and over again, he tells us to seek the lost, take care of those in need, and serve one another generously and graciously. We are God's conduits, his hands and feet and eyes and ears, here on earth. We're blessed when we give to others as he gives to us. Anytime we put our efforts and energies into reaching those in need, our Father is pleased and honored.

> *It is so easy for us to focus our prayers on ourselves. "Thy kingdom come, Thy will be done" keeps us farsighted—attentive to God's agenda first.*

FRESH BREAD

Once we've addressed our Father, honored the fullness of who he is through his many names, and focused on his agenda, then Jesus tells us that it's time to ask God to meet our needs. "Give us this day our daily bread." Notice how comprehensive this request is. We're not merely asking God to be involved in our area of greatest need or sharpest struggle, we're asking him to provide his presence and provision for us in all areas of our lives. Put simply, we should depend on him for everything, regularly. Bread gets stale and spoils if it's not eaten. We need fresh bread on a daily basis.

We tend to focus on the problems, the needs, the deficits, and the trials. But we don't need God's help only when we give the big presentation at work; we need him while we're driving to work, interacting with our assistant, meeting with our boss, talking on the phone, and returning e-mail. Jesus told us to pray in a way that acknowledges our Source. "God, everything I have comes from you. You're my source for all that I'm entrusted to steward. I wouldn't even get to work if you didn't give me breath to wake up this morning. You're my source for *everything*. So, Lord, give me today, and all that I need throughout it."

I love the way Psalm 121 expresses this same idea: "I look up to the mountains—does my help come from there? My help comes from the LORD, who made heaven and earth!" (121:1-2, NLT). Does our help come from our boss or the government or our accountant or our ability to work harder? No. It all comes from God, who made heaven and earth.

SHOCKPROOF

Once we've acknowledged God as the source of all we already have, and once we've trusted him to provide all we need, then Jesus leads us into a critical part of the prayer, a touchy area: "and forgive us our debts, as we forgive our debtors." If we want our lives to be propelled by God's breath and to move forward effortlessly, then our hearts must be right with God and with other people. One of the most liberating, energizing things we can do each day is go to our Father and ask his forgiveness.

In fact, I would encourage you to take it even a step further and pray, as David prayed in the Psalms, for God to search you, know you, and test your sincerity (see Psalm 139:23). Ask him to point out any blind spots or areas that you may not realize need attention. If there's any part of your life that's offensive to the One you love the most, then you surely want to know about it and deal with it.

My fear is that as our culture becomes more desensitized and shockproof, our consciences become looser and more self-justifying. We think, *Hey, times have changed, right? This thing in my life is no big deal—everybody does it now.* We're no longer alarmed by things that we once recognized as sinful, harmful, and dangerous to our relationship with God and our own well-being. For this reason, I encourage you to ask God to keep you sensitive to sin, aware of his ways and not your own or our culture's.

Not only do you need to ask God for forgiveness each day, but you also need to make sure you're right with other people. Jesus basically said, "You'll be forgiven to the degree that you forgive other people" (see Matthew 6:14-15). In the same way that you and I forgive each other, God forgives us. Pretty scary if you think about it! This means that it's vitally important to make deliberate decisions each day about how you're going to treat other people.

That's even true of the people who have been mean to you, ugly to you, spiteful, and harmful. When you pray the way Jesus instructed, you're in effect saying, "God, those people who hurt me need to be forgiven in the same way I have been forgiven by you. So just as you've extended your mercy and forgiveness to me, I offer it to them as well. I want to forgive them, God, and let you take care of avenging and dealing with them wherever they are in their hearts. I'm not going to hold on to grudges, and I'm going to ask that they forgive me for how I've hurt them."

You're not only praying this for those offenses that have already taken place, but also for those that are yet to take place. It's an attitude, an overall approach to the world of being forgiving or, as I like to say, breath-giving. Instead of being fearful of all the mean, nasty, selfish people out in the world, you can show them the love of God because you know that he is big enough to handle their issues. You don't have to do God's job for him and monitor the gates to his Kingdom.

When you let go of judging, condemning, and policing other people and their behavior, you'll discover that you have a lot more energy to devote to your real purpose: loving them and loving God. Paul writes, "Don't let evil conquer you, but conquer evil by doing good" (Romans 12:21, NLT).

You and I must make this decision every day. Otherwise, we begin to feel hurt, offended, sinned against, and then justified for our own sinful behavior in return. Every day we should ask God to forgive us as we adopt a forgiving attitude toward the world.

FIGHTING WORDS

Now we're ready to consider a critical part of the prayer that some people overlook: "and lead us not into temptation, but deliver us from evil." Let me first say that this traditional wording implies a different meaning from the original Greek text. It's more accurately expressed as "God, do not allow me to be led into temptation." It's important to realize that God does not lead us into temptation or set us up for failure. We are actually asking him to help us when temptation comes our way, to give us the power to resist and say no. Jesus is telling us that not only must we seek and grant forgiveness for what has happened in the past, but we must take our stand against the devil and ask God to help us resist his schemes against us in the future.

As we become more comfortable talking to God, we discover that there are different kinds of prayers. It's one thing to say a prayer of blessing or thanks before a meal or to offer a feel-good devotional. But we must also realize that we're in a war with our enemy, and sometimes warfare prayers are required. Scripture is clear about this: "Be strong in the Lord and in his mighty power. Put on the full armor of God, so that you can take your stand against the devil's schemes. . . . And pray in the Spirit on all occasions with all kinds of prayers" (Ephesians 6:10-11, 18). It's not that we have to pray the right prayer so that God will listen or because it works like some magic spell. We pray this way because we realize we're in the midst of a spiritual battle!

There are times for devotional prayer and other times when confrontational prayer is necessary. We must renounce the unholy one and all his fiery arrows and crafty schemes. We must pray for protection around our families and friends, around our homes and churches. We need to consecrate and fortify our marriages and the lives of our children. We must take our stand against the forces of darkness in the name and power of Jesus Christ. Too often we think of prayer as a pleasant, dreamy meditation, but sometimes our prayers should be more like a street fight!

> *Too often we think of prayer as a pleasant, dreamy meditation, but sometimes our prayers should be more like a street fight!*

Maybe you're thinking, *Come on, Chris—is prayer really supposed to be that confrontational? Do we really need to be praying this way every day?* James 5:16 says, "The effectual fervent prayer of a righteous man availeth much" (KJV). When was the last time you prayed fervently? If you want to make a difference with your prayers, then you can't just think of prayer as a time to sit and meditate on happy thoughts for ten minutes. At times, you and I need to confront the devil using the weapons God has given us.

HAPPY ENDINGS

Finally, here are some instructions on ending our conversation time with God. Jesus tells us to put a big old exclamation point at the end of it! "For thine is the kingdom, and the power, and the glory, for ever. Amen." We must have faith in God's ability to act. This phrase reminds us that God can do anything and that he's got everything he needs to accomplish his purposes in our lives.

When I conclude praying, I often like to end with this passage: "This is the confidence we have in approaching God: that if we ask anything according to his will, he hears us. And if we know that he hears us—whatever we ask—we know that we have what we asked of him" (1 John 5:14-15). What a great way to end, right? We have complete and total confidence in our Father, who can do everything he said he would do.

Though I grew up in church, I had no sense of the power of prayer. In fact, I figured it was just another thing Christians did to stay on the good side of God. As a teen attending Bethany World Prayer Center, though, which became my home church in Baton Rouge, I saw what it really looks like to worship God and pray. As I said earlier, Pastor Larry Stockstill led our church through twenty-one days of prayer to begin every year. It was during those seasons that I first witnessed the incredible power that God unleashes when his people join together to connect with him in prayer.

So it made sense that in January 2001—the month before Church of the Highlands held its first service—our launch team would spend twenty-one days seeking God together. And now, every January and August since, our church body has joined together again in 21 Days of Prayer, a time of praying (to connect with God) and fasting (to disconnect from the things of the world—whether it be certain foods, media, or anything that consumes our time and attention).

During these intensive times of prayer, several thousand people meet at our various campuses every weekday morning for an hour of corporate worship and prayer. We are desperate to have God's strength and power behind everything we do, and there is no doubt that the success we've seen is a direct result of this dedicated time of prayer.

If you have the opportunity to pray with other believers, I urge you to take it. Even if you don't, you can still follow Jesus' example. Prayer is simply a conversation with God—spending time talking and listening to the One who made you and loves you most.

BREATHING LESSON

If you want to reinvigorate your conversations with God, I encourage you to make the Lord's Prayer your own. Take each of the seven phrases, putting the idea in your own words and then personalizing it.

Think about how you want to address God in a warm, loving way. Consider which of his names you want to remember and honor. Ask for his will to be done before your own agenda. And when you do ask for your needs to be met, invite God to meet them in all areas of your life, not just the urgent ones. Ask him for forgiveness and ask his help to forgive others in the same way.

Tell him you need him to help you avoid whatever tempts you personally. If you're tempted to go to the mall to shop and overspend, then ask him to help you with that. If you're tempted to chat online with someone you shouldn't, ask him to be with you so that you don't go there. Whatever your temptation is, invite him to strengthen and fortify you. Take a stand against the enemy in your life. And finally, have faith in God's ability to accomplish everything. This fresh air approach will make prayer one of the most enjoyable parts of your day. Amen!

Ask, and it will be given to you; seek, and you will find; knock, and it will be opened to you. For everyone who asks receives, and the one who seeks finds, and to the one who knocks it will be opened. What father among you, if his son asks for a fish, will instead of a fish give him a serpent; or if he asks for an egg, will give him a scorpion? If you then, who are evil, know how to give good gifts to your children, how much more will the heavenly Father give the Holy Spirit to those who ask him!

LUKE 11:9-13, ESV

CHAPTER 8

GOD'S LOVE LANGUAGE

....

A person will worship something. . . . Therefore, it behooves us
to be careful what we worship, for what we are
worshipping we are becoming.
RALPH WALDO EMERSON

When I was growing up, our family sometimes visited relatives, people from church, or friends from my father's work. My mom would always make sure that we kids were all dressed appropriately and give us a refresher course in etiquette. It didn't matter where we were going. She believed there was a set of rules we should follow for how we were supposed to behave once we were actually in someone's home.

This included how to respond if our hosts offered us refreshments or invited us to stay for lunch or supper. Every time we arrived at our destination, just as my father was pulling in the driveway, my mother would say, "Now, remember, if they offer you something to eat or drink, just say, 'No, thank you.'"

And, of course, I would ask, "But, Mom, what if I'm hungry?" or "Even if it's just something to drink?"

She would look at me with one of those mother-type looks that communicate more than can be put into words. "It's not polite," she'd say. To which I couldn't resist asking, "Why not? They're the ones offering." Finally getting a little exasperated (because now we were almost to the front door), she would say, "They're just trying to be nice."

Usually by this time, the people we were there to visit would be welcoming us in and so I'd be quiet. But in my mind, I always wondered, *Why would people just act nice by offering something they don't want to give us?*

Looking back, I realize my mom never wanted us to put anyone out, so she was essentially teaching her children a rote response to a polite question. It was just something we knew to say. In fact, it reminded me of our Sunday morning worship services when the pastor would often say, "We thank the Lord because he has filled us with such joy." I'd always look around (and later, as a teenager, almost start laughing) because what I saw did not in any way resemble joy. Long faces and grim expressions. Downcast eyes and tight, clenched jaws. I had seen joy, and this definitely wasn't it. It just seemed to be a rote response.

SHOW YOUR FEELINGS

I actually liked and respected our pastor a great deal. Yet Sunday worship seemed to consist of either insincere expressions or words spoken or sung without any emotion at all. Maybe you experienced the same thing when you were young and watched most of the worshipers around you showing about as much enthusiasm as they might have waiting in their dentist's office for a root canal.

Growing up, the world was way more fun than anything I'd seen in church. But based on what I understood about the Christian faith from reading the Bible and hearing our pastor preach, it should have been the opposite. I believed then and still maintain that if we're connected to God, the living God who has forgiven our sins and provided a home in heaven for us, then it's truly the Good News, the best news we'll ever hear.

Worship is love expressed. And it seems to me that if we've experienced this great news and encountered God's radical love, then our expressions of love to him will resemble all the other love expressions in our life—not just the sincere love we have for our spouses or the dedicated love we have as parents, but even the unabashed enthusiasm we have for strawberry ice cream or the family dog.

Worship is love expressed.

Seriously, based on our expressions of love alone, some of us seem to love our dog more than God. And football? My goodness, don't even get me started about sports. Or enjoying good food? In case you've forgotten, I live in the South! There's no doubt we all know how to worship, it's just a matter of where it's applied. This is true for all of us.

If we want to experience a breath of fresh air in every area of our lives, then we must get a new perspective on what it means to worship God. When we do, we will experience a blast of wind that will refresh and energize our relationship with him. Before we jump in, keep in mind that worship is not what goes on in the church service, but rather what takes place in our individual hearts. Corporate worship is important. But our love for God must be expressed throughout our lives—every day and in every way. This is what worship is all about.

THE LANGUAGE OF LONGING

Most people are quick to acknowledge that worshiping God is a deeply personal issue. However, I believe we miss the entire point of worship when we reduce it to nothing more than each person's subjective interpretation. If you ask people, "What's the proper expression of worship to God?" you'll likely end up with "Well, we all have our own ways. That's your style and this is my style. That's your tradition and this is mine. You do it your way and I'll do it mine."

Let's challenge this idea. If worship is love expressed, then it seems to me that we need to focus on what the object of our affection wants, not what we like. If I was going to love you, I can't just love you the way I want to love you; I have to love you the way you like being loved. Because of my love for you, I want to focus on you and offer you the things that meet your needs. So to say, "This is just my style or my preference or my tradition" for worshiping God doesn't seem to be a good starting point.

Gary Chapman wrote a book about twenty years ago called *The 5 Love Languages* that remains on bestseller lists to this day.[8] As a pastor and a professional counselor, Chapman wanted to help couples understand each other's needs so that they could have stronger marriages. In the book, he describes five styles of giving and receiving love that apply to all of us. He calls these different styles "love languages" and explains how we can learn to speak in another person's native language as well as help him or her learn our own.

There's the love language grounded in acts of service, which happens to be my love language. If you do something for me, especially something that needs doing or that I don't particularly enjoy doing, that conveys love to me. I don't need touching and gifts as much, but when my wife cooks my favorite meal or when the kids surprise me and do the yard work, I feel loved and appreciated.

My wife, Tammy, on the other hand, really appreciates quality time together. She doesn't care about all the other things as much, but if I just stop during the day and look in her eyes and ask, "Honey, how are you doing today?" she feels special. My willingness to give her some individual time in which I'm fully present and focused on what she needs speaks more than a dozen roses or a beautiful necklace (although I've never had her turn those down).

Speaking of flowers and jewelry, Chapman says that some people speak in the love language of gift giving. (Okay, I confess—I'm glad that's not Tammy's!) My son David is a "stuff" guy. All I have to do is give him something for him to feel loved. If he gets money for his birthday or Christmas, you can bet he'll be at Walmart or the mall within twenty-four hours.

Another love language is spoken through words of affirmation. Some people don't want you to do anything for them or to give anything to them, and they don't necessarily need your time, but they do appreciate constant encouragement. They like to receive frequent feedback from the people around them on how they're doing. They feel loved when they receive the sincere compliments and honest affirmation of their loved ones.

My youngest son, Joseph, thrives on hearing these expressions of love from the rest of us. Our family has a birthday tradition where, during the birthday meal, we go around the table and tell the birthday boy or girl some of the things we like and appreciate most about him or her. Joseph eats this up and can't wait to hear exactly what each one of us will say. I remember that at his last birthday, he didn't even wait for his brother David to finish speaking before he turned to Michael and asked, "Okay, and what about you? What do you like about me?"

The last love language is physical touch or closeness. My daughter, Sarah, who's now a young woman and taller than me, still loves to give and receive hugs. "Daddy, will you hold me?" is one of her favorite requests. The people who speak this language are often the ones we think of as "touchy-feely," the huggers and shoulder patters who need physical closeness in order to feel loved and appreciated.

According to Dr. Chapman, the secret to becoming a great lover of people is learning their primary love language. If we're going to have a great marriage, a great relationship with our kids, even productive relationships at work, then we must discover those individuals' respective love languages and love them that way. It seems to me that if we're going to love God in a way that he likes, then we've got to know his love language. That means that we must let go of focusing on worship as something to make us feel good. How often do we say, "Boy, I really enjoyed the worship service today!" or "I sure got a lot of our worship time this morning"?

God's fresh air blows into our lives when we love him in the way he likes. We must remember that *we don't worship for our benefit but for God's.*

FOR HIS PLEASURE

Scripture tells us that God created us, along with all things, for his pleasure (see Revelation 4:11). Real worship, then, is not about us; it's about him. While God is not a human being, he displays emotions throughout the pages of Scripture. He grieves, gets jealous, gets angry, and feels compassion, pity, sorrow, and sympathy. He loves, delights, rejoices, enjoys, and even laughs. All those expressions are in the Bible. We serve a God with emotions, a God who loves to be loved. We serve a God who has a love language and finds pleasure in our worship.

We don't worship for our benefit but for God's.

And he makes it clear what his love language is throughout the pages of his Word. He says, "Here is what I like. . . ." In fact, he reveals his love language in what just happens to be the longest book in all the Scriptures, the book of Psalms. For reinforcement, when Jesus was asked what the greatest commandment is, he replied, "Love the Lord your God" (Luke 10:27). If you think about it, loving God is the only thing we do now that we know we'll still be doing in heaven.

The word that is used over and over in Scripture to describe what God desires is simply the word *praise*. As we've seen before, nuances of meaning are sometimes lost when translating Hebrew and Greek text into English. This seems especially true when we look at the original words that are summed up by our one word *praise*.

When we read *praise* in our English Bible, it could have been translated from one of seven different words in the original Hebrew. Some of these Hebrew words are polar opposites of one another, yet both end up reduced to the one English word *praise*. Let's consider each of these seven possibilities and their significance in how we worship God. Keep in mind: our goal here is to learn the specifics of God's love language. These seven meanings of *praise* can help us express our love in the ways that he wants.

The first word, *hallel*, is used frequently in Scripture. In fact, it's where we get the word *hallelujah*. *Jah* means "God," so we're proclaiming, "*hallel* God!" when we shout "hallelujah!" *Hallel* means "to boast," "to rave," "to celebrate," even to be "clamorously foolish."

If you've ever been to Tiger Stadium for an LSU football game, you might gain a deep appreciation for *hallel*. Just before the players run onto the field, masses of cheering fans in purple and gold yell, "Geaux Tigers!" The noise level kicks up another notch as the band plays the LSU fight song and the players run out onto the field. It's an exhilarating experience, and that's all just a warm-up for the excitement during the game itself.

You may be thinking, *Really? Are you serious? God wants me to act like I do at a football game? I thought he wants me to be quiet and somber, with my eyes shut and head bowed.* No, it's actually the opposite. "Those who seek the LORD will praise [*hallel*] him" (Psalm 22:26). God enjoys it when we *hallel* him. God enjoys it when we freely express our love and appreciation to him. Let's not worship a piece of leather more than we worship our living God.

The next word is *yadah*, which means to acknowledge someone or something in public with our hands extended. It literally means to raise our hands up toward heaven and acknowledge the greatness of God. This term is used in Psalm 138:1: "I will praise [*yadah*] you, LORD, with all my heart." Notice the way our bodies naturally express what we're feeling in our hearts—a longing, a reaching, a yearning to be closer. When we express our love to another person, our hands are almost always involved. This word, *yadah*, could be used to describe a child reaching up for his mommy or daddy while calling out, "Hold me!"

MORE OF WHAT GOD LIKES

The third word for praise in the Bible is the word *barak* and is used to convey blessing, giving thanks, bowing down, and even kneeling as a sign of humility and gratitude. It's the opposite of our wild and rowdy *hallel*-type praise. It means to honor God by presenting ourselves to him. It means to yield and say, "Here I am, Lord. I'm yours."

Barak means I am going to praise God by presenting my entire self to him: "Praise [*barak*] the LORD, my soul; all my inmost being" (Psalm 103:1).

When we *barak* before the Lord, Scripture tells us that we will receive all of his benefits. When we give ourselves to the Lord as a *barak*-type praise offering, David tells us God forgives all our sin, heals all our diseases, redeems our lives from the pit, crowns us with love and compassion, and satisfies our desires with good things (see vv. 3-5).

Next we find the Hebrew word *zamar*, which literally means to make music to God, or—to be more precise—to make music with stringed instruments before him. Music definitely seems to be a big part of God's love language.

And we don't necessarily have to like the music God likes. I don't listen to loud, jam-out, screamo-type music. I actually like . . . (big secret) classical music. If you check the playlist on my iPod, you'll discover a lot of Beethoven and Mozart. Seriously. But what I like isn't necessarily all that God likes, so when I'm speaking his love language, I find something that I hope pleases him.

God likes it loud. Check out Psalm 150: "Praise him with the sounding of the trumpet, praise him with the harp and lyre, praise him with timbrel and dancing, praise him with the strings and pipe, praise him with the clash of cymbals, praise him with resounding cymbals" (verses 3-5). Notice the repetition there at the end—God not only likes the clash of cymbals, but he likes them resounding over and over again!

The fifth word is *shabach*, and its meaning makes some people uncomfortable. This kind of praise means to shout, to address in a loud tone, to holler. Now I like this one. If I go to a football game on a Saturday, I like to get loud and help pump up our team. God likes it when we get loud and excited as we think about him as well. "Because your love is better than life, my lips will glorify you. I will praise [*shabach*] you as long as I live, and in your name I will lift up my hands" (Psalm 63:3-4). In other words, God's love language is audibly loud. He wants to hear us—and wants us to hear one another.

BETTER THAN FOOTBALL

Our sixth word has a meaning similar to another praise word we just mentioned, with one important distinction. The word *towdah* means to praise God by lifting our hands toward heaven in adoration. However, it's different than the kind of hand-raising denoted by *yadah*. *Towdah* describes lifting our hands in praise receptively, expectantly, waiting for things not yet received. If *yadah* implies us reaching up to God, then *towdah* shows us receiving from God.

There's a sense of "Pour it on me, Lord, I'm ready. I know you're a good God who gives good gifts, and I'm here to worship you today. I came to bless you in your love language, but you keep giving it back because that's just who you are. So here I am—thank you, Lord." In Scripture, we find, "He who offers a sacrifice of thanksgiving [*towdah*] honors Me; and to him who orders his way aright I shall show the salvation of God" (Psalm 50:23, NASB).

Notice that two of the seven praise words involve lifting our hands. If people give you a hard time for having your hands up when you worship publicly, then just tell them that you're talking to God in his love language!

The final word that we translate in English as "praise" is *tehilah*. Psalm 34:1 says: "I will extol the LORD at all times; his praise [*tehilah*] will always be on my lips." *Tehilah* means exuberant singing.

Think about the picture five out of these seven praise words create when combined. Acting clamorously foolish, with hands lifted, playing loud instruments, shouting, and singing exuberantly. Sounds more like an Alabama-Auburn game or a reunion between family members at the airport than the worship at most church services! Wouldn't it be great if Sunday mornings at church were more exciting than Saturday afternoons at the stadium?

WHO'S ON FIRST?

The truth is, every one of us is likely practicing these seven kinds of worship. It's just a question of where you and I are directing our praise. In other words, there's something that you're already exuberant about, lifting your hands in excitement over, and probably getting loud and passionate about from time to time. You are worshiping something or someone now. It's already happening. So really, the question isn't whether you are a worshiper, but what or whom are you worshiping?

Maybe the place to begin getting fresh air in your worship life is not by changing your style of worship but by changing its direction. If your expressions of love go to your dog, your spouse, your football, your house, your hunting, or your shopping, then you're worshiping that person or thing more passionately than God. I'm not saying you can't get excited about your family, your hobbies, or even your possessions. It's just a matter of whether those other things you love reflect God's goodness to you or whether they take his place.

God doesn't want to be a second-rate love in your life. Since he mentions it in the first commandment—"You shall have no other gods before me" (Exodus 20:3)—it's clearly important to him that he come first in your life. Jesus said it this way, "Love the LORD your

God with all your heart, all your soul, all your mind, and all your strength" (Mark 12:30, NLT). He said this was "the most important commandment" (verse 29).

In this statement, Jesus basically gives us a worship checkup self-exam. Here are three areas, Jesus said, that should be focused foremost on loving God. First, he says we should love him with all our heart and soul. How do we do that? If we worship anything with our heart and soul, we give it our affections.[9] This means that we express our love in clear, passionate ways. Some people have told me, "Well, Chris, I do worship God passionately. I just do it privately, in my heart."

If I told my wife something like that . . . well, you can just imagine how it would go over. "Honey, I love you so much, but don't expect any hugs or kisses from me, babe. Uh-huh, I love you in my heart. But I don't hug." That wouldn't go over too well. God wants and needs our affection. If we're capable of worshiping only "in our hearts," then we're withholding ourselves from the One we say we love the most.

HEART AND SOUL

If you look in the Bible, it's clear that a lot of people understood this. David got it. He wrote, "I would rather be a gatekeeper in the house of my God than live the good life in the homes of the wicked" (Psalm 84:10, NLT). Essentially he was saying, "I would do anything to be around you God." Now, David made some huge mistakes in his life and yet God called him "a man after my own heart." God always showed favor to David because David got it. He was a worshiper; he expressed his love. He wrote love poetry to God, he played music for God, he danced for God.

Let's express ourselves and our love for God. Too often, many of us seem afraid to let go and let our love loose before God. I think we've allowed what people think about us determine our expression to God. So when we try to love God with his love language, we look around to see who might be watching, or we base our worship on what everyone else is doing. We focus on our feelings instead of God's.

I want to encourage you to go for it. If you want fresh air in your life, then let yourself get excited about God and your relationship with him. Allow yourself to love him in his love language, in the ways that he has made it known are special to him. Love him with all your heart and soul.

> *If you want fresh air in your life, allow yourself to love God in his love language.*

The second way Jesus asked us to love God, after worshiping with our whole heart and soul, was to worship God with our minds. How in the world do we worship God with our minds? We simply focus our thoughts on God. Consider the way our minds work when we're falling in love with someone. Our beloved is the last one we think about before we go to sleep. He or she is the one we dream about. That person is in our waking thoughts. God wants to preoccupy our minds in the same way.

Whatever you worship, you think about most of the time. If you love golf, you're often thinking, *I wonder if I can fit in a little time at the driving range this afternoon?* If you love shopping, you frequently wonder, *Now what time do those stores close?* If you love football, you know exactly how many days until the season begins. If you go to the website of your favorite team (I confess I go to mine every day), you are likely to find a clock counting down the days, hours, and minutes until the next season's kickoff. I haven't met anyone, myself included, who has that kind of counter showing how long until the next worship service.

Recently I was reading in my home office when my son Jonathan came in. He's sixteen and tall—over six feet—and strong. I looked up and smiled and said, "Hey, buddy, what do you need?" He looked back at me and said, "Nothing. I just thought I'd hang out with you a little while. Was just thinking about you, Dad."

124

Talk about making an old dad feel all mushy inside! How cool is that? My teenage son was thinking about me and just wanted to come and be with me with no real agenda. The message I received is that he loves me. He didn't want anything from me at that time other than to be with me. The Lord revealed something to me during that time with Jonathan. God whispered to me, "Chris, this is worship. And I like it when you just want to be near me. When you just think about me throughout your day, regardless of where you are or what you're doing."

ALWAYS ON MY MIND

So here's the checkup: What do you think about most? What are you thinking about right now? Is it God? Some people, topics, and events will predominate your thoughts today, tonight, tomorrow, the rest of this week, and for weeks to come.

You know that experience you have when you're planning a really great vacation that's long overdue? It may be months away, but your plane tickets are bought, your spouse is already shopping for beachwear for the whole family, and you're all excited just knowing it's coming up. As it gets closer and closer, you think about it more and more. God wants to be on our minds in the same way. He doesn't care if we love golf or look forward to a vacation. He does mind it, though, if he's not on the top of our list.

Finally, Jesus told us to worship God with all of our strength. Every day when people from our congregation volunteer hours of their time to feed people, pass out clothing, refurbish homes, and provide a host of other practical expressions of love for God through the Birmingham Dream Center, God receives it all as worship.

So when you're greeting people at the door on Sundays or leading a small group or showing generosity to a person in need, you're worshiping. When you use your gifts to build something, bake something, sew something, create something in service to God and his

Kingdom, then you're expressing your love to him. This is why I never want anyone at our church to feel pressured or obligated to serve in any way. If someone is not able to offer what they do as a gift of worship, then they shouldn't do it.

My wife likes it when I'm affectionate and show her how much I love her, but she also wants to see how much I love her when I'm out in the backyard mowing the lawn. She needs me to be a yard boy just as much as a lover boy! How you treat the people you love reflects your feelings and expresses your devotion to them. How you expend your human energy and physical strength is a good indicator of what you love. What do you spend most of your time doing? Are you doing it for God? Or for someone, or something, else?

BREATHING LESSON

If you want to experience a breath of fresh air, a real burst of life-giving breath, be willing to worship God in the various ways he appreciates. Examine your affections, your thoughts, and your activities to see where you're directing them. Whatever excites you most in life—be it sports or traveling or spending time with family—should pale in comparison to how passionate you are about God.

I want to encourage you to step outside your comfort zone and worship God in the way the Bible describes—heartfelt and full of expression. When you're willing to worship him in that way, you are letting him and everyone around you know how much you love him. And the result? Well, just try it and see how he refreshes you in return.

The trumpeters and singers performed together
in unison to praise and give thanks to the LORD.
Accompanied by trumpets, cymbals, and other

instruments, they raised their voices and praised the LORD with these words:

"He is good!
His faithful love endures forever!"

At that moment a thick cloud filled the Temple of the LORD.

2 CHRONICLES 5:13, NLT

CHAPTER 9

WHERE EVERYBODY KNOWS YOUR NAME

....

Friendship is born at that moment when one person says to another,
"What! You too? I thought I was the only one."

C. S. LEWIS

A few years ago, Tammy and I were in China on a church missions trip. Our group decided to spend our last day sightseeing. We spent the morning at the Great Wall of China—what an amazing place! It was definitely spectacular.

Because I needed to be back in the States before the rest of the group, Tammy and I had to return to the airport before everyone else. I explained the situation to our friends, and Tammy and I headed back to where we had started the tour. We were already in a cab when I heard someone shouting my name. "Chris! Chris! Over here—you have to see this!"

It was our tour director, a missionary who knew the language and culture quite well. Since we were worried about the time, I said, "Sorry, but we've really got to go—our flight's in only a few hours." We went back and forth like this until he insisted, "Now, I won't take no for an answer. I really have to show you and Tammy something that you absolutely don't want to miss. Grab your bags. You can get going after you see this!"

Annoyed, I let out a big sigh. We grabbed our luggage and trudged over to see what was worth risking being late for our flight. Once I was next to him, the tour director said quietly, "Chris, that wasn't a real cab! It's one of those look-alikes where the driver takes you out into the country, beats the life out of you, steals everything you have, and leaves you for dead. I had to get you out of there without the driver knowing I was on to him." You can imagine how incredibly grateful Tammy and I were to this man for probably saving our lives. He had our backs when we didn't even know we were in danger.

STOPPING SHORT

Each of us needs other people just as much as my wife and I needed someone watching our backs as we prepared to head to the airport in China. For many of us, however, relationships seem just as threatening as a robber waiting to mug us in a back alley. Nothing has the potential to drain our breath and leave us feeling alone and exhausted more than other people. The hurts, the wounds, the bad relationships that drain us of life and breath and energy begin to take a toll and affect all the other areas of our lives. Most people are wounded, and this may be the single greatest area that prevents us from reaching our full potential.

One of the most overlooked stories in the Bible involves the father of our great father in the faith, Abraham. He, too, experienced a painful loss that ended up preventing him from reaching his intended destination. "This is the account of Terah. Terah became the father of Abram, Nahor and Haran. And Haran became the father of Lot. While his father Terah was still alive, Haran died in Ur of the Chaldeans, in the land of his birth" (Genesis 11:27-28).

In the next verses, we see God trying to move in Terah's life, trying to get him to Canaan, the Promised Land. In fact, I wonder if God's original call was to Terah, not Abraham. "Terah took his son Abram, his grandson Lot son of Haran, and his daughter-in-law Sarai, the wife of his son Abram, and together they set out from Ur of the Chaldeans to go to Canaan. But when they came to Haran, they settled there. Terah lived 205 years, and he died in Haran" (Genesis 11:31-32). Although this family moved from their native land toward the land of milk and honey, Canaan, Terah never made it. Perhaps when he and his family reached a city that just so happened to have the same name as his dead son, he couldn't go any farther.

Terah had to pass through Haran in order to go where God was calling him. Once there, I suspect that he must have been reminded of his pain. And he just stopped. He couldn't go on. It was too hard, too painful, too demanding. It seems he could not let go of his grief in order to embrace the joy that lay ahead. He likely could not believe that God was still in control and had not abandoned him. He stopped short based on his own perceptions, rather than pursuing the truth of God's destination. As a result, he never reached the place God wanted to take him.

Like Terah, many of us are shaped by our negative experiences and never overcome them to discover the destiny to which God is calling us. Too often we stop short, refusing to believe that we can catch our breath and enjoy an abundant life. We succumb to fears and false perceptions. The enemy defeats us with lies that bog us down, causing us to lose energy and hope. We get stuck in the doldrums, a dead zone from which we just can't seem to emerge and get back on track.

BAGGAGE CLAIM

Life should come with one of those big signs that you see on ocean beaches, the kind that cautions swimmers to beware of riptides. Only this one would read, "Warning: When we're hurt, we're not very smart." Pain can cause blindness and obstruct objectivity and common sense. Things may look calm on the surface, but a swirling vortex below waits to swallow us up. We let the past define the future and never move on. We think we're doing the right thing, but often we're simply doing whatever alleviates our pain in some way. When we reach debilitating places, as the land of Haran was for Terah, we must allow ourselves to need and to trust the people in our lives.

Certainly, the enemy's lies pollute our other relationships. Terah's decision affected his whole family. In Genesis 12, we see that God had to separate the family. He called Abraham to move on, leave his father's house, and follow God's leading. What an incredibly difficult decision that must have been.

The problem with baggage is that it affects other people's trips. Have you ever been traveling with a group and had one person's lost luggage impact everyone on the tour? You're traveling together, perhaps for a work convention or a church missions trip, maybe a field trip at school or just a vacation with friends. Almost everyone packs light and reduces their luggage to a carry-on. And yet there's the one person who checks two bags and still drags an overstuffed duffel on board. It's bad enough that the entire group has to wait at baggage claim upon arrival, but if the person's luggage gets lost, then it causes delays, frustrations, and disappointment.

The same is true for us. The more baggage we carry with us, the more it slows us down. And our relationships are affected when we can't handle our own issues and constantly force everyone else to deal with them too. Our wounds get transferred to the people close to us. And unless they're vigilant and know how to handle us, our pain becomes contagious and compounds our heartache.

We make decisions that aren't good for us and create defense systems to ensure that we're never hurt in the same way again. We become controlling and rigid, suspicious and skeptical of others' motives. Our insecurities accumulate from an ocean wave into a tsunami of paranoia, fear, and distrust. The most tragic result of unresolved pain is that it can destroy our relationship with God.

After Abram moves on, Terah is never heard from again. His story ends there.

NEVER WALK ALONE

God actually intended people to be a source of life, a community of support and fellowship, taking care of one another. As I shared earlier, I'm fascinated by Paul's shout-out to his friend Onesiphorus, whom he described as a breath of fresh air (2 Timothy 1:16, TLB).

I gained a new appreciation for this kind of friendship when I was preparing to plant Church of the Highlands in 2001. The first thing I did was assemble a team of people who wanted to help me. I called this committed team of thirty-four people the launch team. John Maxwell once said that "it takes teamwork to make the dream work."[10] That is so true. None of us could have even come close to accomplishing individually what we accomplished together. Our shared vision, commitment, and devotion made us better together.

Genuine fellowship, that sense of having a few people in our lives who really know us, accept us, and love us, can make all the difference in the world. A sense of community can make our trials bearable and make our triumphs worth celebrating. We can listen and share, help and encourage, support and be supported.

When we aren't in community, we can quickly find ourselves drifting into the doldrums again. "Let us not give up meeting together, as some are in the habit of doing, but let us encourage one another—and all the more as you see the Day approaching" (Hebrews 10:25). This is not just talking about attending church or even being part of a small group or Bible study. We can attend any gathering of people and still be lonely. We can be surrounded by people and yet feel totally isolated, withholding our hearts and not receiving what others want to offer us.

A sense of community can make our trials bearable and make our triumphs worth celebrating.

Throughout the Bible, we consistently see the importance of being part of a group of people with whom we can be open and honest. Today, most churches call them small groups or community groups and emphasize their importance as the lifeblood of their body. Nonetheless, many of us still walk alone, tripping and limping along instead of walking lockstep on our faith journeys with fellow pilgrims.

Walking alone never works. As much as we want to be self-sufficient and independent, the truth is that we can't find lasting satisfaction in ourselves. We can earn all the money in the world and achieve all kinds of amazing feats, but if we don't have others to share our success with, we're just as empty as we were before we were flush with money and accomplishments. "There was a man all alone; he had neither son nor brother. There was no end to his toil, yet his eyes were not content with his wealth" (Ecclesiastes 4:8).

LONE RANGERS

Since most of us would agree that we need others, why do so many of us try to go it alone? I'm guessing that as soon as you read that question, a dozen reasons immediately sprang to your mind. And I'm also guessing that some are legitimate and that others are just excuses. Let's think through some of these reasons together and explore ways to move beyond them and experience the intimate connections we all crave.

First, there's naïveté. Some people just assume that they must face life alone, and so they never take time to build meaningful relationships. Having never tasted true love and support, the genuine encouragement of other people, they remain independent and naively believe they don't need anyone. Many may even develop a tough exterior and try to bulldoze over the people around them. So often, though, that toughness overlooks the fundamental human need we all have for other people.

There's a story about legendary boxer Muhammad Ali in his

heyday, flying to one of his matches. As the flight attendant went through the safety procedures, she noticed that Ali didn't have his seat belt fastened. The attendant told him that it was mandatory that all passengers be buckled in before takeoff, but still the famous fighter would not comply. He said, "Superman doesn't need a seat belt!" To which the quick-witted flight attendant responded, "Superman doesn't need an airplane either!"

Another reason many people often try to go it alone is because of their temperament. We may blame ourselves and think we're just not cut out to be part of the group because we aren't very outgoing. We avoid those settings where we have to meet new people, telling ourselves, *That's just the way I am.*

If we let them, other people can be truth bearers and remind us of God's grace, love, and compassion.

We convince ourselves that others just won't understand us or accept us. We decide we're not very interesting. The truth, however, is that others are often much more accepting of us than we are of ourselves. We end up condemning ourselves for a variety of reasons and then lose all perspective on what's true and real. Other people can be truth bearers and remind us of God's grace, love, and compassion if we'll let them.

FEAR FACTOR

This leads us to another major barrier: fear. It never gets easier to risk sharing who we are and what we feel unless we practice doing it. As a pastor, I've discovered that no matter how often we talk about the benefits of joining a small group, some people remain intimidated by the thought of joining one. They imagine sitting in a chair in the middle of the room while everyone grills them and picks them apart. They're afraid they'll be put on the spot and exposed for who they really are. And ultimately, like all of us, they're afraid they won't be loved. That others will reject them if they really know them.

This fear is often based on past experiences where we were, in fact, rejected, abandoned, or abused by other people. Many of us have been burned in the past. And the effects can linger many years after the offense, so much so that we vow to ourselves that we will never let that happen to us again. We commit to never needing anyone and never allowing ourselves to be vulnerable and transparent for fear of showing our weaknesses, for fear of revealing things that will be used against us.

This fear of telling others our secrets reminds me of a men's group I heard about. These three guys were good friends and had been meeting for prayer and Bible study for a while, but each had a secret. As they got to know one another over time, one guy finally said, "Guys, I've got to tell you something. I'm really wrestling with lust and looking at online porn. . . . It's just so easy to click and find it anytime. I really need your prayers and your help in defeating this habit."

The second guy said, "Wow, I really appreciate your honesty—thanks for being real. Since you were, I might as well tell you guys the truth as well. I'm a gambling addict, and I've put my family in serious debt. I take huge risks on the stock market, play online poker, and go to the casino every chance I get. I need your help to beat the odds and overcome this thing."

The third guy looked at his two friends and said, "Well, guys, I'll confess as well. I really struggle with gossip, and I can't wait until I get out of here!"

Seriously, most of us fear that someone will tell our secrets and betray our confidence. We're terrified of what people might think if we reveal our darkest struggles. It just seems so much safer not to let people know. They'll only betray us, right? So why put ourselves in that position when we can just keep them at arm's length by smiling and saying, "I'm just fine—and how are you?"

There's a reason that our enemy attacks our relationships: he knows wounds caused by others can be some of the harshest, most debilitating injuries we will ever face. Being betrayed by another person is absolutely one of the worst things that we can experience. Whether that betrayal comes from a parent or a teacher, from a best friend's gossiping tongue or from the keyboard of our spouse's laptop, we feel crushed and powerless. Pain is part of every relationship, but we get to choose whether it's the deadening pain of separation or the growing pains of reconciliation.

> There's a reason our enemy attacks our relationships: he knows wounds caused by others can be some of the most debilitating injuries we will ever face.

NONE OF YOUR BUSYNESS

Another reason we give for going it alone is busyness. We say, "Well, of course I'd love to have closer relationships and more time for my family and friends. There's just so much going on right now. Maybe when things settle down. . . ." But they never do settle down, do they? We've let the world set the agenda for us.

In our overstimulated world, which bombards us with constant information, entertainment, and education opportunities, we can always point to something we feel obligated to do. So many of us paralyze ourselves in the doldrums because we're tired and burned out from overworking and only rarely allow ourselves to relax and unplug. When we're busy, we wish we could slow down. When we try to slow down, our minds are preoccupied with all the work we've left undone, all the things waiting for us when we return. So we bounce back and forth like Ping-Pong balls, never experiencing rest or the soul refreshment that real relationships can give us.

While I love social media and appreciate the ways it allows us to communicate and connect, I also fear that it gives us a false sense of relationship. We post what we want others to see on our Facebook page, we Twitter and text, we e-mail and chat, but we don't slow down long enough to sit across from people so we can look them in the eye and listen to their hearts. We don't slow down enough to reveal ourselves to them in person.

If you're serious about wanting fresh air in your life, then I encourage you to reprioritize your life as necessary to make authentic relationships a deliberate commitment on your part. Charles Swindoll summed it up well:

> *Nobody is a whole team. . . . We need each other. You need someone and someone needs you. Isolated islands we're not. To make this thing called life work, we've got to lean and support. Relate and respond. Give and take. Confess and forgive. Reach out and embrace. Since none of us is a whole, independent, self-sufficient, super-capable, all-powerful hotshot, let's quit acting like we are. Life's lonely enough without our playing that silly role. The game is over. Let's link up."[11]*

CHEERS

God never intended for us to walk through life alone. And deep down, we know it. When the Lord saw that Adam was alone in the Garden, he observed that it is not good for man to be alone. So he created Eve, and from them came the first family, the first community. And, yes, just like us, they had their issues after making their fateful choice to bite the apple of disobedient discontent. But our longing for connection, for friendship, for relationship is still inside us, a foundational part of every human being.

A longing for connection, for friendship, for relationship is a foundational part of every human being.

You remember the classic sitcom *Cheers*, set in a Boston tavern? Its theme song articulates a very simple message that clearly resonates with us all: "Sometimes you want to go where everybody knows your name, and they're always glad you came. . . . You wanna go where everybody knows your name."[12] We want to be known and recognized; we want a place where we belong. We want to be able to trust other people and know that they relate to us without judgment. We want to experience relationships that give us life and put our problems in perspective.

It seems to me that the place where we can find a supportive community should be our local church, not the corner bar! Unfortunately, there's often more joy, support, fellowship, and encouragement in a neighborhood pub than in a church small group.

This is not the way God intended it to be. There should be more acceptance, more safety, more encouragement in our relationships with other believers than anywhere else.

Since the beginning of Church of the Highlands, we've deliberately created a place where knowing your name is a priority for everyone. We've been more than a church with big weekend services. We've been a church made up of small groups of people doing life together.

Whether they meet in homes, parks, restaurants, college dorm rooms, or offices, these groups form the heart and soul of who we are as the body of Christ. By the way, these groups aren't intended to be just another church event or something to fill a slot on people's calendars. Our vision is for everyone to be part of a group with other individuals who are willing to grow in their faith together, to support one another, to encourage one another, and to celebrate with one another.

Such groups reflect Paul's desire for believers: "So it is with Christ's body. We are many parts of one body, and we all belong to each other" (Romans 12:5, NLT). We need people in our lives who are willing to share in the good and the bad, the ups and the downs. In the second year of our church, a man in one of our small groups had cancer and lost all his hair to chemo. While the group members offered all kinds of practical support, one of the most moving things the other men did was to shave their heads too. They wanted their friend to know they were standing with him.

No one should have to deal with a disease like cancer alone. No one should have to sit in a hospital waiting room alone while their spouse or child or parent is in surgery. No one should have to wait for test results to a biopsy alone. No one should have to stand at an open grave alone. No one should have to go through a divorce alone. We need each other.

NEIGHBORHOOD WATCH

Years ago, our church brought in someone to lead our staff through the DISC personality assessment. Before we took the test, the presenter taught us about four aspects of our interactions with other people. The first is the public face we put forward, how others see us and how we see ourselves. If we were to describe this part of ourselves, we might say, "I know and you know." This is the face we all see.

But allowing others into our lives is scary and challenging and intimidating. So we create the second aspect—masks, areas of our lives where "I know but you don't know." We all have those parts of ourselves that no one knows. Our secrets. Our past hurts and wounds and scars. Our deepest fears and insecurities. Our special hopes and dreams. While we think it feels safer to walk alone than to reveal these parts of ourselves, the truth is that we're never safe if no one knows us.

But living life with a mask on doesn't work. This is why Paul writes, "We refuse to wear masks and play games. . . . Rather, we keep everything we do and say out in the open" (2 Corinthians 4:2, THE MESSAGE). Removing our masks is one of the secrets to getting rid of habitual sin. Certainly, God forgives us our sins, but in order to find healing we need to let someone else know too. We're told, "Confess your sins to each other and pray for each other so that you may be healed" (James 5:16, NLT).

We all need the kind of accountability where others are watching over our souls and we're watching out for them. Not so we can all become self-righteous chaperones policing each other's behavior, but so we can get our sin outside ourselves and see its effect on our lives and on the lives of others. When no one knows what we are doing, we're not safe.

Removing our masks is one of the secrets to getting rid of habitual sin.

We tell ourselves that we can be anonymous, that no one will get hurt, that no one will find out. But whatever we do secretly—whether it's drinking or stealing or watching porn or going places we shouldn't go—separates us from God and other people. And this separation will only grow the longer we keep our secrets.

As the saying goes, "You're only as sick as your secrets." If we want to be healthy and whole, if we want fresh air in our lives, then someone needs to know what's really going on in our lives. Much of the time, we need the protection of others more than we even realize.

When we go on vacation, many of us ask someone to watch our house, maybe even to house-sit. We want someone to protect our possessions, to take care of our pets, and to maintain our obligations. How much more, then, do we need others who will watch out for our souls as we travel through life? Real community provides a neighborhood watch for the soul.

SEEING THE BLIND SIDE

My wife and I have signals we use between us when we're together in public. You know, in case one of us has spinach in his teeth or needs a tissue for her nose. That's a good illustration of the third aspect of our lives: those things we don't know about ourselves but that others do. Even though we think we know ourselves well, even the most self-aware person can't see their blind spots. No matter how polite, how well-educated, how fit, how wealthy, or how charming each of us may be, we still can never fully know ourselves.

Our enemy loves to exploit our blind spots: to tempt us, to shame us, to frustrate us, to trip us up. Every day he's devising ways to get us to fail. We usually don't recognize him, because if we did, we would flee into our Father's arms. Instead, the devil waits for us to turn our backs, to look the other way, to get preoccupied with other distractions so that he can attack us where we're most vulnerable. His attempts usually work best when we're trying to go it alone. A wolf won't attack an entire flock of sheep. No, he waits for a straggler; a loner; a weaker, slower lamb who's fallen behind.

The reality is that we need people to be honest with us. Think about this for a moment. Who is speaking into your life with total and complete honesty? Telling you the things that are hard to hear, that they know you may not want to hear? It has to be someone you trust, or else you'll dismiss that person's observations or insights. And in order for trust to grow, you have to be committed over time to helping each other. "Faithful are the wounds of a friend, but the kisses of an enemy are deceitful" (Proverbs 27:6, NKJV).

JOIN THE TEAM

Finally, there's the aspect of our untapped potential. This is the part of us that we can't see and that others can't see. Only God sees it. He alone knows what's inside us, and he wants us to mature and grow and develop into all that he created us to be. All of us have unrealized potential, and we will never reach our full potential alone. We need others to help us discover and utilize all the gifts we've been given. My potential as a pastor was never realized until I discovered my team. You'll always do more and accomplish more as part of a team.

Golf is a lonely sport—just you and the course. But there's a game you can play with a team called "scramble." Each foursome gets to choose which player's shot they will count, and then they all hit from that spot for the next stroke. Each player contributes in the area of his or her strength—whether hitting from the tee or putting—and each one benefits from the others' strengths. An old Zambian proverb sums it up well: "When you run alone, you run fast. But when you run together, you run far."

Who's on your team? Who knows your dreams? Who knows you well enough to glimpse your potential as it emerges? Who can nurture and encourage you for the distance so that you become the person you were meant to be? We need people who will help grow us into who we really are.

Jesus certainly modeled this kind of selective relational investment by choosing only twelve disciples. He didn't want to start a religious movement or go on a world tour. He chose twelve other men, none of them anywhere near perfect, and shared his life, his heart, and his love of God with them. He wants us to pursue the same kind of intimacy today. He wants us to bring a breath of fresh air to every relationship we have and, in turn, to be refreshed ourselves.

BREATHING LESSON

God created you to draw support from others and to be a source of life to other people. But you need more than just another dozen friends on Facebook or another handful who follow you on Twitter. You need more than just the people at the office in the cubicles around you. You need more than just the group of guys you work out with or the group of ladies in your book club.

Whether you like it or not, God's plan to keep you out of the doldrums involves other people. He wants you to connect to him and to his people. To do so, you'll need to move past Haran (your past hurts and disappointments) and develop meaningful relationships. You'll never fully get the wind back in your sails until you do.

Take a moment to assess the relationships in your life. Who

really knows you? Who gets you? What risks do you need to take and what secrets do you need to share in order to improve the quality of your relationships? Certainly, you want to be discerning and thoughtful about which people you trust. The integrity of your friends is far more important than the number of friends you have.

> A man of many companions may come to ruin, but
> there is a friend who sticks closer than a brother.
> PROVERBS 18:24

CHAPTER 10

MONEY MATTERS

··

Money never made a man happy yet, nor will it. The more a man
has, the more he wants. Instead of filling a vacuum, it makes one.

BENJAMIN FRANKLIN

My dad was my hero. He was the best man at my wedding. He was instrumental in helping me start Church of the Highlands here in Birmingham. After a brave battle with cancer, he went to be with the Lord on June 29, 2010. I miss him more than any words can describe.

My dad made his living as a numbers guy, serving as a legislative auditor for the State of Louisiana for most of his career. He retired in his midfifties with full retirement benefits after his decades of service. In 2000, when I announced that I was moving to Birmingham to plant a church, he and Mom decided it was time to make their own announcement. After talking about it for a while, they had decided to move from Baton Rouge too. They were going to buy a recreational vehicle and spend the rest of their lives traveling the country, living in America's most beautiful parks as "full-timers," as such nomads are called in the RV world.

My parents decided their first stop would be Birmingham so

they could help me launch the church and set up the financial systems and controls before moving on to tour the country. And that's exactly what they did, with one exception. Dad and Mom parked their RV at Oak Mountain State Park just outside of Birmingham and served seven days a week as accountant and secretary for the newly formed Church of the Highlands. However, they never made it out of Alabama. Mom and Dad fell in love with Birmingham and Church of the Highlands and never visited another park. In fact, they sold their RV, bought a home in Birmingham, and continued to serve our church.

My dad was a financial genius. The systems and controls he set up for our church were done through the lens of an auditor—not an accountant or attorney. Auditors see things differently. They make sure every "i" is dotted and every "t" is crossed. Dad implemented values and practices that God honored and our people appreciated. To many people who had watched and experienced other churches, his financial integrity was like a breath of fresh air.

Dad always taught me that God's heart is that of a giver—just think of John 3:16. It was natural, then, for us to model generosity at the Highlands from the beginning. That is why we give away everything—notebooks for message notes, CDs, etc. We tell our congregation that they can't buy these things because they already paid for them through their tithes and offerings.

It has also been important to our leadership team that we gain the respect of our people by leveraging the money they give. Rather than simply giving to missions, for instance, we have joined with other congregations to plant churches that also give to missions.[13] Partnering together, we've been able to contribute millions of dollars—far more than our church could have given on our own.

My father's influence is evident in many more practices at the Church of the Highlands. His dedication was unbelievable, even after being diagnosed with cancer in 2008. While he battled the cancer that had developed in a tumor on the side of his head, just behind his right eye, he never missed a day of work. Even through thirty-seven rounds of radiation, he remained positive, hopeful, and productive. He was brave, honest, and the hardest-working person I have ever met. His legacy and the lessons he deposited live on in my life and in the life of each person who is touched by our church.

PRINCIPLE NOT PRESSURE

As I reflect back on the many nuggets of wisdom from my dad, one seems to sum up his entire approach to life. Dad said, "Live by principle—not pressure." And the result of that wisdom in his own life, in our family, and then in our church was more than evident. There was freedom—wind in the sails of his life that transported all of us to a fuller, richer, more faith-filled life.

From my experience, most people can't say that about their lives, especially in the areas of money and time. The world around us tells us we must look good to get ahead, which often leads us to spend money we don't have and invest time in pursuits that bring us only temporary comfort or prestige. Often we have little left over in either area for God or our family, and our relationships feel stagnant or strained as a result.

So many of us are on financial life support, barely making ends meet and holding our breath every month to see if we have enough to pay the bills and meet our expenses. Our financial lives end up leaving us like someone struggling with asthma; we're gasping for air and laboring over each breath. "Give careful thought to your ways. You have planted much, but harvested little. You eat, but never have enough. You drink, but never have your fill. You put on clothes, but are not warm. You earn wages, only to put them in a purse with holes in it" (Haggai 1:5-6).

Unfortunately, money seems to be one of the greatest sources of pain, worry, and anxiety in our lives—not only on an individual level, but more and more on a community, state, national, and global level. We see all kinds of financial unrest, from collapsed economies of entire countries to the economic recession that's plagued our own nation the past few years. People want solutions; they want change and a new way of dealing with the issues of debt, credit, wealth, and poverty.

And it makes sense that people are tired of the way money matters control their lives. Basically, when it comes to money, we're not free—we're in bondage. We're in trouble as a nation. We're in trouble around the world. We have more abundance than ever before in history and yet we're less satisfied. The toll of worry, stress, and anxiety that millions of people experience because they're in debt up to their eyeballs only continues.

PIERCING PROSPERITY

Certainly, these problems didn't happen overnight. It's a cycle that's been going on for generations. Every culture has fought for their freedom and independence. Once freedom is achieved, the by-product is prosperity. And this is where the problem begins, as I see it, because most people don't know how to handle material abundance.

Prosperity stirs up greed. Statistically, it's been demonstrated that the more a person's income increases, the less they give away. Shouldn't it be the other way around? Yes, there are certainly wealthy, generous individuals who give away healthy percentages of their net worth, but most people become greedier when they make more money. They get ahead, but it's never enough.

We also reach into the future to have more now. Despite what we know about the economy and our own personal finances, many people continue to borrow more and more, spending far beyond their income. Though consumer borrowing rates fell fairly sharply during the Great Recession, they shot back up in late 2011, a sign that Americans tend to revert to borrowing when the economy improves.[14] So we go from freedom to prosperity, from prosperity to greed, and then from greed to bondage. We're miserable and feel trapped, on an endless treadmill from which there seems to be no escape. And this is not a new phenomenon. Scripture describes this cycle in a way that's as timely as any headline you see in the news.

> Godliness with contentment is great gain. For we brought
> nothing into the world, and we can take nothing out of it. But
> if we have food and clothing, we will be content with that.
> Those who want to get rich fall into temptation and a trap
> and into many foolish and harmful desires that plunge people
> into ruin and destruction. For the love of money is a root of
> all kinds of evil. Some people, eager for money, have wandered
> from the faith and pierced themselves with many griefs.
>
> I TIMOTHY 6:6-10

We've become pierced by our own faulty decisions, blinded by our desire to have all that we want right now, no matter what it steals from our future. In order to experience a breath of fresh air in our finances, perhaps it's time for a new way of thinking. We must cultivate an attitude of contentment and maintain practices that give life.

We go from freedom to prosperity, from prosperity to greed, and then from greed to bondage.

My father taught me four values and three complementary practices, all based on God's Word, that can move you out of the fury of the financial storm in which you're sailing and into calm waters. These values and their applications can put wind in your sails once again.

FULL DISCLOSURE

The first value is integrity. You must be willing to take an honest look in the mirror and make a truthful inventory. The process of change begins with your own personal disciplines. "So then, men ought to regard us as servants of Christ and as those entrusted with the secret things of God. Now it is required that those who have been given a trust must prove faithful" (1 Corinthians 4:1-2).

A healthy financial culture begins with each individual. Every nation, institution, or home is just an extension of the people in them. If an individual provides a firm foundation based on integrity, then the organization is poised to flourish. If an individual builds a structure based on greed and deceit, then the organization is sure to wither and die.

God knows how you handle your finances behind closed doors. And other people are watching as well. Regardless of the spin you might try to place on your decisions, your actions show what you value. That's why the apostle Paul said, "We want to avoid any criticism of the way we administer this liberal gift. For we are taking pains to do what is right, not only in the eyes of the Lord but also in the eyes of man" (2 Corinthians 8:20-21).

Think about it this way: if your family's expenditures for the year were printed for the public to see, what would embarrass you the most? How would you feel if everybody knew about your personal budget, debt, and giving? Most people would be embarrassed about some area of their finances if it were made public.

The same applies to churches and other organizations. Often, people want to be more generous but grow skeptical and cynical about how the resources they give are being used. They want the methods and purposes used by the organizations to which they give to reflect honesty, integrity, and genuine values.

A reputation of integrity is built with transparency and accountability. Most organizations are not required by law to disclose their financial statements unless they're in trouble or suspected of breaking the law. But fully disclosing financial records shows that you have nothing to hide and that all your practices are honorable, fair, and ethical. There are no gray areas hidden between the red numbers and the black ones.

In our personal lives, we must maintain the same standards of integrity in all dimensions of our finances. If we can't afford something, we need to stick to our budget and plan for a time when it's within range. If we owe taxes to the state and federal governments, we must pay them and not try to omit any facts about our income. If a sales-clerk makes an error in our favor, we should tell him or her as soon as we realize it and return the money. These kinds of choices show integrity. God is watching us, and he wants to bless us. Let's not stand in his way.

> *God is watching us, and he wants to bless us. Let's not stand in his way.*

GENEROUS TO A FAULT

The second value my dad taught me is stewardship. *Steward* is the Old English word for "manager." When we steward our finances, then, we manage them in a way that pleases God, who owns it all. We must develop responsibility and accountability in all of our practices, recognizing that how we spend our money is so much bigger than what we purchase, charge on our credit cards, or deposit in the bank. Everything we have comes from God—everything, down to each breath we take.

One of the most life-giving things we can do is get rid of an "owner mentality." When one hand holds tight to what we have while our other hand grabs for more, we never receive the gifts that God wants to give us. We must be openhanded in our approach to all that we're given: our possessions, our homes, our salaries, our cars, our property. The goal of life is not to accumulate wealth and possessions.

Our purpose in life is to handle God's resources as faithful managers, good stewards who look beyond the immediate personal effect of a decision and are guided instead by eternal principles. "Whoever can be trusted with very little can also be trusted with much, and whoever is dishonest with very little will also be dishonest with much. So if you have not been trustworthy in handling worldly wealth, who will trust you with true riches?" (Luke 16:10-11).

The third value I learned is generosity. We must live to give. We are conduits of God's extravagant love and abundant provision. We are blessed to bless others. "Just as you excel in everything—in faith, in speech, in knowledge, in complete earnestness and in your love for us—see that you also excel in this grace of giving" (2 Corinthians 8:7).

I challenge you to be known for your generosity. Give things away. Don't focus on how much you can make and spend or even save. Focus on how much you can give away. And remember that money is not the only thing we can give. We can share our talents, hugs, smiles, and prayers. God not only models this kind of amazing generosity to us, but he makes it clear in his Word that our attitude about giving impacts our lives. "Remember this: Whoever sows sparingly will also reap sparingly, and whoever sows generously will also reap generously. Each of you should give what you have decided in your heart to give, not reluctantly or under compulsion, for God loves a cheerful giver" (2 Corinthians 9:6-7). Since this is true, shouldn't we be looking to give away as much as we can?

And make no mistake—it's okay to have things, to enjoy possessions, to want certain items. I don't believe in an ascetic gospel, that we must literally withhold and impoverish ourselves in order to prove our faith is genuine. Some people believe the only way to be holy is to sell everything, and yet this can become just as misguided and all-consuming as acquiring everything.

It's all a matter of where our hearts are. When our focus is on acquiring, getting, earning, achieving, accumulating, and hoarding, we lose our spiritual focus on God. In Psalm 62, David makes this contrast clear and direct: "Do not trust in extortion or take pride in stolen goods; though your riches increase, do not set your heart on them" (verse 10).

We must rest and remain anchored to God alone. We must not trust in our riches or set our hearts on increasing them. It's not wrong to have things; it's only wrong when things have us. We need to rejoice in what God has made and given to us. But we shouldn't set our hearts on those things and demand them or make them the goal. If we make loving God and serving others our objective, then there will be no pain involved in giving away what we have. We'll have a deeper abiding joy that's not tied to what we own or anything money can buy.

This is why I'm convinced that the best antidote when our hearts have drifted to the wrong place is generosity. Nothing breaks the spirit of materialism like generosity. We'll never go wrong if we keep remembering what our Master has made so clear:

> *It's not wrong to have things; it's only wrong when things have us.*

"You're far happier giving than getting" (Acts 20:35, THE MESSAGE).

Exercise a generous heart—one that gives more than money and possessions. Sometimes it's easier to write a check than to give something of ourselves. For instance, you might spend time with someone just to enjoy his or her company, or phone someone to say you're thinking of and praying for him or her that day. Give your talents to serve others. Giving your attention and affection can be so simple and yet can make such a huge difference in another person's life. A timely hug can communicate more than any material gift you might give. Do you need a breath of fresh air? Here is a promise from God's Word: "The generous will prosper; those who refresh others will themselves be refreshed" (Proverbs 11:25, NLT).

SEED MONEY

Finally, we must focus on the eternal impact we all can make with our resources. If we want to obey God and to experience a breath of fresh air in our finances, then we must focus on treasures in heaven. Think about the return on your investments. Remember the parable of the talents? The master goes away and gives each of his servants a number of talents to invest. When he returns and inquires about what they've done with what he gave them, the first two servants tell him how they made wise investments and multiplied the returns. However, the third servant blew it! He buried his talents and did nothing with them whatsoever. It's clear that God wants a return on all that he has given us:

> God is able to make all grace abound to you, so that in all
> things at all times, having all that you need, you will abound
> in every good work. As it is written: "He has scattered
> abroad his gifts to the poor; his righteousness endures
> forever." Now he who supplies seed to the sower and bread
> for food will also supply and increase your store of seed
> and will enlarge the harvest of your righteousness. You will
> be made rich in every way so that you can be generous on
> every occasion, and through us your generosity will result in
> thanksgiving to God.
>
> 2 CORINTHIANS 9:8-11

God gives talents to his people in order that his investments might grow. He gives seed to the sower in hopes of multiplying the harvest. He's looking for harvest-minded people who aren't going to hoard the seeds he gives them but instead will plant wisely and produce in abundance. This is the strategy of the great commission, the call placed on all who believe and trust Jesus with their lives to share this Good News with everyone everywhere.

The bottom line of any accounts ledger should be on eternity— not short-term, material profits. The purpose of money is to use it to grow the Kingdom of God. Everything we do must be focused on the harvest. This is God's priority, and it should be ours as well.

"Do not store up for yourselves treasures on earth, where moth and rust destroy, and where thieves break in and steal. But store up for yourselves treasures in heaven. . . . For where your treasure is, there your heart will be also" (Matthew 6:19-21).

FIRST THINGS FIRST

Now that we've looked at the four values—integrity, stewardship, generosity, and a focus on eternal impact—let's consider the practices that put these principles into action. Let's begin with the practice of tithing. This is a simple practice, but one that trips up so many people.

The first portion of everything we receive, a *tithe* as Scripture calls it, belongs to the Lord our God. People usually consider the tithe to be one-tenth of the whole of what we have, but I believe that the principle of tithing centers more on giving to God first rather than giving him a certain amount. The tithe is not just a percentage principle but a principle of firsts. It's an opportunity to declare who means the most to us and what we consider the most important priority in our lives. It's holy to the Lord, and he alone has the power to bless the rest of what we have.

Some people say that tithing is a "law principle," something that was instituted during the time of Moses and done away with after Christ's coming, but we need to realize that this practice shows up at least 2,500 years before the Levitical law was established. I see it first in the sacrifices offered by Cain and Abel, the sons of Adam and Eve. They each offered God something, and he was pleased with one offering but not with the other. Why? What was the difference? Let's look at the account and pay attention to the distinction between Cain's offering, which God did not find acceptable, and Abel's offering, which God accepted.

Abel kept flocks, and Cain worked the soil. In the course of time Cain brought some of the fruits of the soil as an

offering to the LORD. But Abel brought fat portions from
some of the firstborn of his flock. The LORD looked with
favor on Abel and his offering, but on Cain and his offering
he did not look with favor.

GENESIS 4:2-5

Abel brought the firstborn of his flock; Cain did not bring his
firstfruits. God cannot accept an offering if it's not the first portion.
We show our respect and appreciation to him by honoring him first.

Growing up, I learned from my dad early on what tithing meant.
No matter how much money I received, whether an allowance or a
ten dollar bill inside a birthday card from my grandparents, my father
always said, "Give the first to God and then think about the rest."
I'll be honest: I've always experienced unexplainable favor in my life
with money and material possessions. I believe when we honor God
first, he does indeed bless us, not as a quid pro quo transaction, but
because he knows where our hearts are. He knows we're dedicated
to advancing his Kingdom with our resources. He doesn't want our
stuff; God wants you and me. He wants to know where we place him
on our list of priorities.

Tithing is a barometer of where our hearts are, a test to see if we're
serious about trusting God and acknowledging him as the Source
of everything we have. We put God first by giving him the first
of everything (not just money, but everything) because first things
reveal where our treasure is. If we give him the first of our year, it
says something to him. If we give him the first of our week, it speaks
volumes. If we give him the first of our day, it's loud and clear. If we
give him the first of our possessions, it shows we're serious about our
commitment to him.

Although *tithe* literally means "tenth" or "tenth part," this percentage is used only as an equalizer so that we can participate equally
and know we're giving God our first portions. We can't give equal

amounts, but we can all give the first tenth of whatever we have. "A tithe of everything from the land, whether grain from the soil or fruit from the trees, belongs to the LORD; it is holy to the LORD" (Leviticus 27:30). It's possible to give 10 percent and not be tithing. That's because tithing is not giving one out of ten things; it's giving the first of the ten before using the other nine.

The whole point of tithing is to give to God first. "The purpose of tithing is to teach you always to put God first in your lives" (Deuteronomy 14:23, TLB). God obligates himself to bless first things and make them holy. He bestows first things with the power to bless the rest. "In all your ways submit to him. . . . Honor the LORD with your wealth, with the firstfruits of all your crops; then your barns will be filled to overflowing, and your vats will brim over with new wine" (Proverbs 3:6, 9-10).

THE SPACE BETWEEN

The second practice, margin, provides us with breathing room in our finances. Margin is simply the space between ourselves and our limits.[15] It allows room in between where we are now and where we will be in the future. Once again, it's a practice that looks beyond immediate gratification and convenience: "The wise store up choice food and olive oil, but fools gulp theirs down" (Proverbs 21:20).

Margin enables us to say yes to unexpected opportunities that God places before us, while giving us the freedom to say no to opportunities that don't fit his plans for our lives. It helps us endure lean times with confidence. And margin works in every area. If we plan to show up fifteen minutes earlier than each meeting or appointment, we'll arrive prepared and punctual, rather than rushing and stressing about getting there. We'll have more peace in our lives. We don't have to drive faster to make up lost time because we're not late. We can relax throughout the day knowing that our margins protect us from the storms that can come up.

We use the principle of margin in our home, and it's allowed us to continue breathing easy over and over again. You can imagine how hectic a morning can be with five kids getting ready for school. So we encourage everyone to be dressed and ready to go out the door fifteen minutes before it's time to leave. We meet in the kitchen and just hang out, discussing the day ahead, planning beyond it. Everyone's relaxed and unstressed, and we begin the day with peace.

Margin enables us to say yes to unexpected opportunities that God places before us, while giving us the freedom to say no to opportunities that don't fit his plans for our lives.

If we apply margin to our finances, then we can experience amazing peace in that area as well. If we set some money aside for emergencies, then we won't freak out when the car breaks down or our roof leaks. If we have a plan for the long run, then we can relax in the short term. Margin reflects good stewardship.

THE MYTH OF MORE

Speaking of a plan for the long run, finding the discipline to follow our budget is our third practice. We must set ceilings on our expenditures and then stick to them. Having a budget gives us a compass to help us navigate each day's expenses and opportunities. When we stay on budget, we remain on course for where we want to be: unstressed, responsible, peace-filled, and secure. Budgetary discipline provides ongoing reassurance that we're living for God and not for things.

Incidentally, most people see budgets as restrictive. I've found the opposite to be true—even when it comes to our church's budget. At Church of the Highlands, our budget never exceeds 90 percent of the previous year's income. Since our giving increases each year, providing that margin not only takes off much of the pressure, it also enables us to say yes to a lot of proposals. When our staff knows that we have the resources to fund worthy initiatives, that brings a lot of life and fresh air to what they're seeking to do for the Kingdom.

The Bible has been focused on budgets for over three thousand years. You'll remember our friend King Solomon, the son of David and one of the richest and wisest men who ever lived. As he described in Ecclesiastes, he denied himself no pleasure and yet found himself miserable. Basically, he discovered that things can never satisfy the heart.

We're back to the law of diminishing returns: the more we have, the less it satisfies us. You see this every year at Christmastime. Everyone wants to make this holiday bigger, better, and more special than last year's. With all the pressure from advertisers with sales and special promotions, it's no wonder we think we must spend more to make it better. The only problem is that so many people still have not paid for last year's holiday!

One of Solomon's wise observations resonates today more than ever: "Those who love money will never have enough" (Ecclesiastes 5:10, NLT). We see this in families, businesses, even churches—everyone wants more than they have. Why has our nation's debt tripled and quadrupled in recent years? The more we spend, the more we want to spend.

The myth of more would have us believe that more stuff will satisfy us, even after we've already experienced numerous disappointments. I had a good laugh recently when I called and canceled a magazine subscription, only to have a telemarketer call me an hour later with an offer to resubscribe! Did they really think that I would have changed my mind in that hour? Solomon wrote, "The more you have, the more people come to help you spend it" (Ecclesiastes 5:11, NLT).

The great irony of wealth is that it can make our lives seem easier or more pleasurable, but it can't bring us peace, joy, or a genuine love for other people. Oh, it might buy us some rent-a-friends for a while. But money can't improve our marriages or heal a sick child. It can't provide us with the intimacy of loving another person.

In fact, having more money and possessions can actually rob us of whatever peace we might have had. That's because when we own more stuff, we have more stuff to worry about. We have to worry about maintenance and upkeep, repairs and emergencies, theft and accidents. We have to spend money on all those worries as well, either through insurance or services to maintain the beloved possession. While we'd think that people with more money would have less stress, just the opposite is true: "The rich seldom get a good night's sleep" (Ecclesiastes 5:12, NLT).

The solution is to live by principle, within your means, by following a plan that reflects your priorities and values. Don't buy into the myth of more—literally! Don't buy into the world's other practices either. I've seen big problems develop in churches when they adopt certain practices from the world of corporate culture. Building campaigns, fund-raisers, faith promises—we don't do them at our church. Honestly, I think most people hate them—the pressure, the obligation, the unspoken messages sent by such endeavors. I think if you stick with God's plan for raising money, then you have nothing to worry about. So we don't ask people for money. We ask God for what we need and trust him to convey the need to his people.

THE PRINCIPLE OF PEACE

As we conclude thinking through how we can learn to breathe again in the area of our finances, let me point out an interesting insight that I first heard from my friend Pastor Craig Groeschel. "Prince" is the root of the word *principles*. The implication is that principles were originally royal decrees that all the subjects of the land had to obey.

One of the names given to Jesus is "Prince of Peace." You may recall it from a familiar Christmas verse: "For to us a child is born, to us a son is given, and the government will be on his shoulders. And he will be called Wonderful Counselor, Mighty God, Everlasting Father, Prince of Peace" (Isaiah 9:6). The Hebrew phrase for "Prince of Peace" is *sar shalom*. In Hebrew, *sar* means the one in charge, the lord of the land, the chief, the general. It's not just royalty like Prince Charming; it's much more authoritative. It's where we get the title *czar* that was used for Roman emperors and later for Russian emperors.

Shalom may be more familiar. It means rest, tranquility, wholeness, completeness, contentment. So together, the two words *sar shalom* can also be translated accurately as "Captain of Completeness" or "General of Tranquility" or "Chief of Wholeness" or even "Lord of Contentment." And if Jesus is all these things, if he is indeed the Lord of Peace, then we must realize that there is no peace if he is not our Lord.

The relationship between these two words—*peace* and *Lord*—and their impact on our lives are fundamental to having fresh air in all areas of our lives. I'm always amazed that some people think they can do whatever they please and then wonder why they don't have peace in their lives. They make immoral decisions and then pray to have peace. They yell at their spouse and kids and wonder why there's no peace at home. They charge up all their credit cards, never tithe, and wonder how they can have financial peace as described in the Bible.

So much of the stress in our lives comes from not following Jesus' principles, which were given for our own well-being. The solution is simple but not easy. We must get under his lordship and make him the Prince of Peace in our lives.

When it comes to money, following his principles brings peace. These are not just good ideas or practical business models. They're not just wise sayings or clever instructions. They are principles, royal decrees, from the King of kings and the Prince of Peace. God wants to bless us, not so we can have a worry-free life of luxury and affluence, but so he can bless us with something far more precious: his peace, his joy, his contentment. What he wants to give us is, indeed, priceless.

BREATHING LESSON

A breath of fresh air in finances begins with values—principles. When you have solid biblical principles, then you can live by principle instead of pressure. After you settle in on the principles that guide your life, then you can begin to work on the practices. You may have to start slow, but start now and you'll immediately begin to sense some wind in your sails.

Change one thing today about how you relate to your money. It may be giving to someone who needs it, giving God what is his, or choosing not to purchase something you don't really need. If budgets and big-picture strategies seem overwhelming right now, pray and ask God to show you just one thing to change about how you relate to your money.

Remember this—a farmer who plants only a few seeds will get a small crop. But the one who plants generously will get a generous crop. You must each decide in your heart how much to give. And don't give reluctantly or in response to pressure. "For God loves a person who gives cheerfully." And God will generously provide all you need. Then you will always have everything you need and plenty left over to share with others.

2 CORINTHIANS 9:6-8, NLT

CHAPTER 11

ROOM TO REST

A field that has rested gives a bountiful crop.
OVID

I recently took my first sabbatical, an extended break of eight weeks intended to provide rest to my body, mind, and soul. For years, my friends in ministry as well as mentors (especially those older than me) had advised me to take one, not just a mini-version or one in name only, but a genuine Sabbath season that would give me room to rest away from all my usual responsibilities and commitments. Honestly, I didn't think I needed one. I've always enjoyed ministry—in fact, it even energizes me. I've always believed in that saying, "If you love what you do, you'll never work a day in your life."

Besides, I had regularly taken a weekly Sabbath day off and was consistent about using it for a day of rest. Since Sunday is my hardest workday—I preach as many as five times—I usually take Monday as my day off. I've always joked that Lionel Richie couldn't have written his hit song "Easy Like Sunday Morning" if he'd been a pastor. Instead it would've ended up being "Easy Like Monday Morning."

I love my days off and start those mornings doing what I do most every day. I grab a cup of coffee and my Bible and spend some time with God in prayer and worship. Then I usually watch some online church services from a list of over a dozen of my ministry friends around the nation. I actually open my Bible and take notes, just as if I were a member of their congregation. I always tell people, "I go to church on Mondays." It's been a great routine that really feeds me.

But 2011 was different. After the death of my father in 2010 and my father-in-law in early 2011, and after twenty-eight years of ministry and ten years of "pedal-to-the-metal" church planting, ministry growing, and team leading, I was tired. Deep-down tired, emotionally exhausted, the kind of tired you don't even realize is there because you've grown so used to it and to pressing on through it day after day.

Our church leadership team saw it in me. Our overseers, an external board of five senior pastors who cover me personally; our trustees, an internal board of seven members who oversee the church business; and our elders all agreed that it was time for me to take an extended break—an eight-week sabbatical.

At first I was hesitant. I'd never been out of the pulpit for more than two consecutive weekends. Would the church be okay without me that long? Or a deeper, scarier question: Would I be okay without my role at the church for that long? What would I do for eight weeks? But the more I thought about it, the more I knew I needed it, and so I began to work with my team and the church to prepare for my two months away.

REST LIKE YOU MEAN IT

My sabbatical was wonderful—life-changing and life-giving. I never read an e-mail, I never answered a phone call, and my golf game improved—well, at least a little. During the eight weeks, I spent four weeks at home, two weeks with my wife in Italy celebrating our twenty-fifth wedding anniversary (a "bucket list" trip for which we'd saved a long time), and two weeks on the Gulf Coast with Tammy and our kids. It couldn't have been better or come at a better time.

Since then, a number of people have asked me what I learned while away. I sometimes jokingly tell them that I learned absolutely nothing, because if I'd learned something then it wouldn't have been a sabbatical. But that's not true. I learned many things—about myself, about God, about my family, and about what's needed for most of us to experience an ongoing sense of God's refreshment in our lives. While they were not the lessons I expected to learn, here are the three big things I learned during that time away.

First, it took me three weeks before I completely disconnected from my responsibilities at work, three weeks before I went an entire day without wondering and worrying about how things were going at the church without me there. You may have experienced that frustration on vacation before, that sense of taking one week of vacation to unplug from the office and another week to ramp back up for when you go back. Of course, it isn't much of a vacation if you spend the entire time either recovering from work or gearing up to go back to work. I thought I was good at separating myself from work when I wasn't there, but the truth is that I thought about it most of the time, even when I didn't realize my thoughts had been drifting to work.

The second thing I learned is that I had lost my ability to recognize when I was tired. I'd learned how to run on adrenaline and push through it. After my sabbatical ended, I began to notice how tired I felt. But then I realized that I wasn't any more tired now than I had been before taking a break. The difference was that I'd learned how to listen to my body during the sabbatical, to recognize and respect my own need for true rest.

Finally, I realized that I needed to make some type of commitment—daily, weekly, monthly, and annually—to intentionally and deliberately rest. I needed a comprehensive life routine that included rest as a key component. Since my sabbatical, I've put a system into place that includes the crucial rest time my mind, body, and soul require in order to remain healthy, balanced, and in touch with God's leading.[16]

NOTHING DOING

I'm not the only one who was overdue for a sabbatical and a commitment to real rest. The truth is that all of us are probably more tired than we realize or want to admit. And this deep sense of fatigue may be robbing us of joy and siphoning off our energy. We may be in the doldrums and have no breath of life filling our sails because we've never stopped our ship to rest and recalibrate ourselves in the direction of True North.

Think honestly about your life right now. Do you ever get tired just thinking of all that you've got to do today, this week, this month? Do you feel just as tired on Monday morning as you do on Friday afternoon? With today's high-pressure lifestyle, not only may you feel physically fatigued, you may run out of emotional, mental, and spiritual energy as well. Call it "depression" or "burnout" or "the blahs" or whatever you want to label it, but those feelings are telling you something.

Like the warning light on our car's dash informing us that we're running low on fuel or need maintenance soon, these personal indicators are there to remind us to rest. We need balance in our lives or we lose our sense of direction and find ourselves forced to stop because we've run out of fuel or broken down. If we don't take rest seriously, then we'll be forced to learn its vital significance the hard way. We can't function without rest; it's simply the way we're made. So often we look for ways to relax or unwind that aren't healthy and find ourselves developing bad habits that ultimately make us even more exhausted.

Interestingly, when Jesus described some of the signs of the end times to his followers, he warned about a hurried lifestyle, the kind of lifestyle many of us live today. He said, "Be careful, or your hearts will be weighed down with dissipation, drunkenness and the anxieties of life, and that day will close on you unexpectedly like a trap" (Luke 21:34). A heart that is dulled or heavy with dissipation is one that is running on empty without even realizing it. On the one hand, it is anxious about life's demands; on the other, it is careless and out of control, like someone who is drunk.

Jesus said to be on guard against getting stretched to the limit. When our bodies and emotions are pulled every which way and stretched to the breaking point, the risk of making sinful choices climbs off the chart. When we get tired and depleted, exhausted and run down, we no longer think straight or with a long-term perspective. We have less clarity about our priorities and what we're really committed to in our lives.

> *A heart that is running on empty is, on the one hand, anxious about life's demands; on the other, it is careless and out of control.*

I saw this problem illustrated in vivid ways when I was a youth pastor in Colorado years ago. Our church would organize frequent ski trips where, inevitably, someone would get hurt. And it wasn't just that they got hurt—there seemed to be a pattern as to when they got hurt. In almost every case, the injury or accident took place in the last hour of the day, during the final run down the slope. People's muscles would be so tired, yet by this time, they had lost their initial hesitancy and were often overconfident in their ability to think fast or stop quickly. So invariably, they fell, crashed, or lost control.

The same is true for you. If you want to experience a breath of fresh air in your life, then you have to resist the temptation to keep going at the same pace all the time. In fact, I have three warnings for you to help you pay attention and realize your own need for rest.

First, beware of overestimating your ability to endure a heavy load or hectic pace. Your personal pride may shame you into pushing through when you really need to rest. "Go on," your ego whispers, "don't be a wimp. You can do it. You can handle it. Keep going. Only losers need rest." Workaholics have such a deep-seated sense of pride that they no longer even hear their bodies' cries for rest. You and I are not superheroes. We're not God. We're human. And we need rest.

Sometimes we give our bosses and family members too much power over what we do, allowing them to push us beyond healthy limits. If we are constantly on call, either at work or as a caregiver for an ill family member, we may need to be honest with others about what we can actually handle.

Next, beware of out-of-control schedules that do not include a firm margin for rest. (Remember that *margin* simply means space between ourselves and our limits; something held in reserve for unanticipated situations.) Very few people say that they have plenty of time to do the things they need and want to do. Instead they feel pulled and pushed, obligated and committed, forced by habit into fulfilling the urgent agendas of everyone around them. Most of the activities on our schedules do not contribute to the vision or goals we've set for our lives. And yet we keep doing them. Over and over and over again, we stay on the merry-go-round of constant busyness, one thing after another. More meetings, more errands, more trips, more phone calls, more e-mails, more chores. But no rest.

My third warning is to beware of substitute solutions. Most people know they need rest in their lives, but they try to fix the problem with a short-term solution rather than the one that God gave us. They think, *Well, I'll take a half-day off* when they know that it will be consumed by playing catch-up on all the other things demanding their time and attention. They think, *I'll just take a sleeping pill* or *I'll just have a drink to relax.* Instead of taking time away for real body and soul rest, they rely on a placebo, a substitute. The problem is, there is no substitute for true rest.

IT'S THE PRINCIPLE THAT COUNTS

God's Word is clear: one of the main ways he designed for us to be refreshed is by honoring the Sabbath. And please realize that the Sabbath is a principle, not a specific day. It's not a law requiring us to honor the seventh day, as some people might think. It's simply a truth about how we're made and what we really need. "It will be a sign between me and the Israelites forever, for in six days the LORD made the heavens and the earth, and on the seventh day he rested and was *refreshed*" (Exodus 31:17, emphasis mine).

Some people say that keeping the Sabbath was simply part of Old Testament law. But what we must realize is that all of God's laws were designed with our well-being in mind. The motivation behind a law is what we should be focused on, not the external logistics of how it's exercised. If we're doing anything just because God said to do it, our obedience can easily become legalistic. We end up going through the motions just like the Pharisees, the religious leaders of Jesus' day who acted certain ways so that they could be smugly self-righteous. In their hearts, they clearly were not focused on loving God but on manipulating God's principles for their own agendas.

God provides us with principles from his Word to give us his abundant life. When we obey those principles, not just the semantics of the law, then his rules become life-giving truth. So often religion gets it backward and tells us we have to serve the day. Yet God gave us the Sabbath for our own good. Jesus certainly made it clear that keeping the Sabbath was never intended to be a rule but a way of life: "He said to them, 'The Sabbath was made for man, not man for the Sabbath'" (Mark 2:27).

To understand this day of rest, we need to understand the origin of the word and the concept behind it. The word *Sabbath* was derived from the Hebrew word *shabbat*, which comes from the Hebrew verb *shavat*. Both words refer to a stop in the normal routine, to actively and deliberately cease function. It's a concept, not a day on the calendar. The idea means taking one day out of seven to stop doing what we've been doing and focus on restoration, relaxation, and renewal.

So the idea of Sabbath is to stop working for wages and competing for rewards. Stop running and going and striving and doing and just be. When was the last time you weren't worried about what time it was? When was the last time you weren't on the clock? Maybe for some of us, a real way to honor and enjoy the Sabbath would be to go a whole day each week without looking at our watches.

Sabbath is about playing and relaxing. Reading and studying spiritual material—not because you have to but because you want to. Taking leisurely strolls outdoors and enjoying the beauty of God's creation. Talking and enjoying the company of your family. Attending church services and worshiping with others. Praying and meditating. Spending time with God without feeling obligated or rushed. Just hanging out together.

While part of your Sabbath may be spent alone, it wasn't necessarily intended to be experienced alone. Sabbath is not just personal but communal. It's about helping one another remember to relax and rest, to enjoy one another without a formal purpose, agenda, or production-minded motive.

At the heart of it, Sabbath is a day to celebrate our freedom from human rules and regulations and to remember our real purpose: to love God and to serve his Kingdom. Why is this so vital to our well-being? As we conquer and create all week long, we can easily develop an inflated and self-centered idea of our own power, our own self-sufficiency. The Sabbath is a constant reminder that for one day a week, we are dispensable to work and to the world but not to our families, our community, or to God.

Like the tithe, the Sabbath principle demonstrates that, by

honoring God's design, we can get more done with less. We can get more out of 90 percent of our income when we tithe than we can from 100 percent when we don't. We can get more out of six days of work and responsibilities than we can if we try to stay on duty all seven days.

The first mention of the Sabbath in Scripture raises some interesting theological questions. "By the seventh day God had finished the work he had been doing; so on the seventh day he rested from all his work. Then God blessed the seventh day and made it holy, because on it he rested from all the work of creating that he had

Sabbath is a day to celebrate our freedom from human regulations and to remember our real purpose: to love God and to serve his Kingdom.

done" (Genesis 2:2-3). First, why does an all-powerful God need to rest? If he's omnipotent, how could he be tired and need to take a day off?

This passage translated literally means, "He was refreshed." And, along with the fact that we don't see God taking a day of rest anywhere else in Scripture, that leads me to believe that God clearly did not need this for himself but did it to set an example for us.

It's important to note as well that the Sabbath day actually comes first and not last. Although it shows up last in the Creation account, God establishes it for us as something to be done first. When I was in Israel recently, I was surprised to learn that the Jewish people mark the start of each new day at sundown. In other words, they begin their day with rest! As someone there told me, "If you rest well, you'll never get tired."

So often we rest only when we are extremely tired or have passed our limits, but God wants us to rest regularly and make it a priority so we won't get exhausted. We're not supposed to take a Sabbath after a long, hard week. We're supposed to take it first thing so we're rested and equipped to be as productive and focused as possible.

WORK TO REST

It takes a lot of work to rest in our world today. That sounds a bit contradictory, but we must make every effort to get the real rest our bodies, minds, and souls need. We must be vigilant and deliberate to ensure that we get what God established as essential to our ongoing welfare. "Let us, therefore, make every effort to enter that rest, so that no one will fall by following their example of disobedience" (Hebrews 4:11).

Many of us need to relearn how to slow down and come to a complete soul standstill. We must reorder our lives and start being intentional about taking care of ourselves in godly, life-giving ways. Resting is not being lazy or shirking our duties. Again, the irony is that we're actually much more productive when we regularly include rest in our schedules than when we keep pushing ourselves and trying to do it all.

Many of us need to relearn how to slow down and come to a complete soul standstill.

Incorporating Sabbath as an active part of your life will require you to set firm boundaries and honor them. You must be intentional about it. You should include holy days in your schedule and even holy moments throughout your day. (The word *holy* simply means "set apart," and that's what I mean here.) If you don't deliberately designate certain times to rest and spend with God and your family, you're unlikely to do it. More "urgent" matters will always demand your attention if you let them.

Maybe a regular date night with your spouse is part of what it means for you to keep the Sabbath. Or it could be a regular time with God each day, as well as a special time once a week or once a month. Maybe you need to make special family celebrations a way to honor the Sabbath as well. It's so easy to give our families what's left over in our lives instead of the primary attention they deserve.

In a basic way, including Sabbath in your life may mean looking at your priorities and revising your usual schedule and routines. Maybe you need more margin in your life so that you're not always running late, stressed to the max, and trying to cram in one more thing each day. Maybe it's time to give your most important activities the best part of your day. Maybe it's time to put the important things first. "In vain you rise early and stay up late, toiling for food to eat—for he grants sleep to those he loves" (Psalm 127:2).

We simply must not ignore God's call to rest. In the Bible, we see an entire generation who didn't enter the Promised Land simply because they had not learned to honor and practice God's ways:

> That is why the Holy Spirit says, "Today when you hear
> his voice, don't harden your hearts as Israel did when they
> rebelled, when they tested me in the wilderness. There your
> ancestors tested and tried my patience, even though they saw
> my miracles for forty years. So I was angry with them, and I
> said, 'Their hearts always turn away from me. They refuse to
> do what I tell them.' So in my anger I took an oath: 'They
> will never enter my place of rest.'"
> HEBREWS 3:7-11, NLT

Clearly, the people of Israel wouldn't listen to the warning signs. They did their own thing and ignored what God had established for their own benefit. I think God gives us the same warning today, but most of us are not listening. Yet if we ignore God's call for rest, we're going to get to the end of our lives and regret our hurried lifestyle. Worse, we are likely to realize we have little of eternal value to show for it.

If we're not careful, our bodies will force us to come to a grinding halt. Our mortal bodies have limitations and need to be honored and respected and appreciated as the temples in which God's Spirit lives. So often we just keep pushing and pushing, though. We rush from thing to thing, crisis to crisis, urgent deadline to urgent deadline, without realizing the toll it's taking on us.

A pastor friend of mine told me about a recent tour he took to Israel. While outside Jerusalem, my friend saw a flock of sheep, but no one was leading it. Then he saw someone behind the flock and assumed it must be the shepherd. Still, that contradicted everything he knew from the Bible about shepherds leading the flock and the sheep following the shepherd's voice. So my friend asked his tour guide why that particular shepherd was following the flock instead of leading it, and the guide said, "Oh, that's not the shepherd. That's the butcher!"

Our shepherd leads us. Our butchers drive us to our own destruction. In one of the best known and most memorized passages of Scripture, Psalm 23, we're told that the Lord is our shepherd and that he leads us beside still and quiet waters. He restores our soul and breathes fresh air into our lives. He wants us calm and peaceful, joyful and rested—not panicked and running from the butcher behind us.

REST STOP

In addition to being something we must work at, rest also requires our faith. Real rest doesn't come from a day off or even from taking a vacation or sabbatical. It comes when our souls are connected to God's power. It comes when our minds relax because we know God is in charge. It comes when we're not stressed since we're trusting God to guide and lead us. Rest comes from our genuine reliance on God to meet all our needs each day. "We see that because of their unbelief they were not able to enter his rest" (Hebrews 3:19, NLT).

Real rest comes when our souls are connected to God's power.

As people of faith, we're not bound by the dimensions of this world. A day of rest allows us to get that "heavenly" perspective, to get away from the natural and into the supernatural. When we have faith, we can remain calm and contented, but when we don't have faith, then we worry and fret and get anxious over every little thing.

It takes faith to obey and to do what we don't fully understand or want to do—including to rest. And even though we have to work at it, finding rest is not hard because the real secret to rest is to get close to Jesus.

Jesus knew what it was like to need rest and to set time aside so that he could be renewed and refreshed, both by spending time with his disciples and time alone with his Father. He often urged his disciples to get away from the crowds with him: he knew they needed to come apart before they came apart. "Because so many people were coming and going that they did not even have a chance to eat, he said to them, 'Come with me by yourselves to a quiet place and get some rest'" (Mark 6:31).

The pressure on Jesus' disciples took its toll, and the same is true for you and me today. Fortunately, his offer is the same today as well. "Jesus said, 'Come to me, all of you who are weary and carry heavy burdens, and I will give you rest. Take my yoke upon you. Let me teach you, because I am humble and gentle at heart, and you will find rest for your souls. For my yoke is easy to bear, and the burden I give you is light'" (Matthew 11:28-30, NLT).

TAKE MY YOKE

It's important to realize here that Jesus doesn't want us to stop producing. In fact, he encourages us to find true rest by taking on another yoke—his yoke. Used as an attachment to the harness on oxen or donkeys, a yoke was made of wood and kept the animals plowing down the same row in the right direction. Once again, it seems odd or contradictory to think that we rest by taking on a yoke, something designed to force an animal to work. But notice that Jesus says, "Take my yoke" (Matthew 11:29)—in other words, we've got the wrong one on. There's a way to be purposeful in our work without growing weary and exhausting ourselves. We simply have to go to him and carry only what he gives us to carry—and nothing more.

In order to experience the refreshment that comes from practicing the principle of Sabbath rest, I recommend four strategies. The first is simply the practice of stopping at regular intervals even if you don't feel tired or think you need the rest. Some people claim that they "work hard and play hard," which is great, but playing hard is not the same thing as Sabbath rest. Part of our rest must be a time of becoming still before God and acknowledging our love of and reliance on him. "Be still, and know that I am God" (Psalm 46:10).

Second, allow your body time to rest by removing external distractions and interruptions. We're so overstimulated in our world today. A friend of mine and I were having coffee recently, and during our conversation he kept checking e-mail and texting on his smartphone. Finally, I said, "I thought this was your day off." He looked at me sheepishly and said, "Well, it is. This is a much slower pace for me than usual."

With all the missiles of media and technology constantly bombarding us, it's no wonder we suffer from societal ADD. Real rest requires times of silence, a fast from the normal ways we communicate and interface with the world. I encourage you to take one day a week to unplug—no e-mail, no texts, no phone calls unless it's an emergency. Let your body and mind rest from the constant influx of information.

Third, I recommend a deliberate plan for embracing your community of family and friends and engaging them in a time of worshiping God together. It doesn't have to be a formal church service or Bible study. It can simply be gathering around the old piano and singing some worship songs together. It can be a time of discussing what you're thankful for that day around the dinner table. It can be a weekly time where you share prayer requests and praises with a group of friends. Coming together as a family and a community and worshiping God restores us more than we realize. We get a bigger picture than just our own lives and can focus on what God is doing in the lives of others we care about.

Finally, in order to practice Sabbath in a way that will refresh you, I encourage you to learn the art of celebration. Feasting is what it's often called in the Bible—times when all the stops are pulled out and you gather everyone together to celebrate a special occasion, a rare event, an amazing achievement, or simply the fact that you're all together in one place. Special activities feed the soul and allow us to step outside the challenges and responsibilities of everyday life. Certainly, Christmas and Easter afford us wonderful opportunities to celebrate and feast together, but we must do this more than twice a year. These don't need to be elaborate affairs, either—just times to acknowledge the beautiful and good in our lives.

The reality is that rest is essential. God knew this when he made us and demonstrated its value to us so that we would grasp just how important it is. Going at full tilt is the way of the world. Striving, working, hustling, and hurrying are supposedly required if we want to get ahead in life. But God tells us that if we want to experience real momentum and life-giving breath in our lives, then we must practice the principle of the Sabbath. "The LORD replied, 'My Presence will go with you, and I will give you rest'" (Exodus 33:14).

We must do everything we can to do nothing. God has promised us that when we do, then we will be refreshed.

BREATHING LESSON

Chances are, if you're like most people, you really needed to hear the message in this chapter. I hope it's been life-giving and refreshing to you, but I want to challenge you to do more than just think about what you want to do differently. I challenge you to do something about it—today. I truly believe that this principle is God's remedy for burnout.

So take the first step right now. If nothing else, stop where you are and close your eyes and just breathe for sixty seconds. If you can do it for five whole minutes, then all the better. Next go and look at your calendar or appointment app or wherever you keep your schedule. What needs to change in order for you to incorporate and practice Sabbath in your life?

I encourage you to set aside time every morning—even for just ten minutes—to refocus your spirit on God, your soul on his Word, and your life on the things that really matter.

Finally, I challenge you to unplug one whole day this coming week and use that time to be present with your family, doing something you love—cooking a great meal together, going for a walk in the park, playing a board game. I think you'll discover that these times of rest and reflection are often the most productive moments of your week.

Teach us to number our days and recognize how few they are; help us to spend them as we should.

PSALM 90:12, TLB

PART 3

FINDING THE SOURCE OF BREATH

CHAPTER 12

THE SOURCE OF BREATH

....

The answer, my friend, is blowin' in the wind,
the answer is blowin' in the wind.

BOB DYLAN

By now, I hope you're convinced that a life totally refreshed with wind in your sails is more than possible. But I realize you may be a little frustrated, too. Perhaps you're beginning to understand the breath-of-fresh-air concept and its application, but you're still not sure how to live it out every day. To some degree, you can learn to live a better life by trying harder, being more focused and organized, and developing healthier habits. However, these changes provide only limited results.

The greatest discovery I made when I was going through the doldrums was that the root of my problem was spiritual, even though my struggles appeared to be physical and circumstantial. I think we often forget that here on earth we are spiritual beings who have a mind, will, and emotions (the soul) and live in a body. We are not physical beings having temporary spiritual experiences. We are spiritual beings having temporary physical experiences on planet Earth.

That's why I'm convinced that, for everything we face, we must deal with it first spiritually. Please understand that I'm not saying we should neglect physical checkups, medical treatment, and visits to doctors and counselors. I believe in using all the practical resources that God provides for us to heal and experience a breath of fresh air.

However, if we recognize we are spiritual beings and address our problems first from this perspective, we may discover a lifelong solution. In my case, I had drifted from a sense of purpose and an intimate connection with God, and I had ended up in a pit of despair. I recognized that I needed more than encouraging words and new habits. I needed a transformed life.

You and I don't have to settle for a mediocre life or try harder to be a "good Christian." God has provided us with a continual power source, best friend, trail guide, and direct link to him. He never intended for us to make life work through our own efforts. He's always wanted to be intimately involved with our lives. This is the very reason he sent his Son to earth to live as a man and defeat death once and for all. With this victory, Jesus gave us a gift, an ongoing breath of fresh air in our lives.

God never intended for us to make life work through our own efforts. He's always wanted to be intimately involved with our lives.

Are you ready for the "big reveal" of this book? If you're a fan of reality TV makeover shows, then you know the big reveal is the moment at the end when we finally get to see the newly remodeled home with all the latest appliances or the slimmed down, glamorized person with the new haircut and wardrobe. It's when we see how all the pieces fit together to produce the total transformation, a coming together of details in order to fulfill the potential of the original.

You may not be surprised by my big reveal here: the source of the blast of life-breath in us is the Holy Spirit of God. You may have even heard or read other explanations of the Holy Spirit in your life, and

I hope they were helpful. Most of the time, however, I'm concerned that we misunderstand and misperceive the gift God has given us in the Holy Spirit. In these final three brief chapters, I invite you to rethink what you've been taught or just assumed about the Holy Spirit. My hope is that you can gain a more accurate understanding of the Spirit's role in your life and a more intimate experience of his presence.

BREATH OF HEAVEN

The word *Spirit* is mentioned more than eight hundred times in Scripture, so obviously it's crucial to understand its meaning and how it's used. Our English translations use one word, *Spirit*, but there are actually two different words and two concepts conveyed in the original languages. In the Old Testament, the Hebrew word is *ruwach*, which literally means "a violent exhalation, a blast of breath, a strong wind." We find it used in the second verse of the Bible: "Now the earth was formless and empty, darkness was over the surface of the deep, and the Spirit of God was hovering over the waters" (Genesis 1:2).

Have you ever been to a lake or pond to watch the sunrise? It's still dark outside and there's no wind; the surface of the water looks like glass. Then suddenly a mighty wind whips around the hillside over the water, sending ripples and waves across to the shore. This is a miniature version of what I think it must've been like at the beginning of Creation.

Imagine this dark, murky body of water with God's breath hovering over it, perhaps stirring up the surface with its force. His breath seems to be the very energy force from which he created everything—earth, heavens, oceans, land, animals, fish, sun, moon, stars, and of course, the first man and first woman, Adam and Eve. It's pretty amazing to think that every created thing began with the breath of God.

In the New Testament, the Greek word for this same kind of breath is *pneuma*, which also conveys a breath or wind, a current of air, a strong breeze. It, too, usually gets translated into English as "spirit," referring to the Holy Spirit, the spiritual friend who comes alongside us and empowers us with God's presence. "The Spirit [*pneuma*—breath] gives life; the flesh counts for nothing. The words I have spoken to you are spirit [*pneuma*—breath] and they are life" (John 6:63).

So every time you read the word *Spirit* in Scripture, it means "breath." Both *ruwach* and *pneuma* carry a sense of force, an active, living energy that blows in and brings life. And this is exactly what the Holy Spirit came to do—breathe new life into us. God doesn't care about our "religious experiences" as much as he cares about giving us an abundance of spiritual fresh air. Too often, we reduce our faith to an airless, stagnant exercise that we try to do perfectly, yet we never feel we have the ability, the energy, or the power to achieve it. We're trying to sail out of the doldrums but don't know where to find the wind.

AS THE WIND BLOWS

If the best word to describe the Holy Spirit is breath or wind, let's consider the implications. Most of us feel more comfortable with things we can see and touch than things we sense or feel on the inside. Many people are uncomfortable with the notion of the Holy Spirit because they want something or someone they can relate to face-to-face as another person. While this is understandable, we must remember that it takes faith to be in relationship with God.

In order to receive his breath of life, we must live by faith and live faithfully. That means being comfortable with the unknown, the unseen, the things we don't understand. But the necessity of faith doesn't mean that the Spirit should remain some vague, mysterious, abstract aspect of God that's beyond our understanding. If we think through the characteristics of wind, we can gain a clearer, more concrete idea of who the Spirit is and his role in our lives.

WIND IS UNSEEN

To begin with, wind is something we feel and experience but don't see. While we can observe its effects and see its impact on leaves and trees, kites and windmills, we never actually see the wind itself. But the fact that we can't see it doesn't keep us from acknowledging it as a reality.

Similarly, we must realize that while the Spirit can't be seen, he can be felt, experienced, and observed in action. When our church was still meeting at a high school, I remember standing at the door after one particular Sunday morning service, shaking hands and talking with people as they left, when a man said something I'll never forget. When I asked this first-time visitor if he had enjoyed the service, he got a funny look on his face and said, "Preacher, there was something in that room today . . . something different."

While the Spirit can't be seen, he can be felt, experienced, and observed in action.

He didn't know what it was—he couldn't see it—but it drew him back the next week. Simply put, it was the presence of God. The Spirit is undeniable, real, and refreshing. We get frustrated sometimes because we can't quantify and objectify the Spirit; we can't catch him and take him apart and study him in a scientific way. Instead, we must rely on faith. And the Bible defines faith this way: "Faith is being sure of what we hope for and certain of what we do not see" (Hebrews 11:1).

After Jesus was resurrected, he appeared several times to various disciples. One of these guys, doubting Thomas, heard from his friends that Jesus was alive again, but Thomas needed to see Jesus for himself before he could believe it. "The other disciples told him, 'We have seen the Lord!' But he said to them, 'Unless I see the nail marks in his hands and put my finger where the nails were, and put my hand into his side, I will not believe'" (John 20:25).

So Jesus gave his disciple what he asked for:

He said to Thomas, "Put your finger here; see my hands. Reach out your hand and put it into my side. Stop doubting and believe." Thomas said to him, "My Lord and my God!" Then Jesus told him, "Because you have seen me, you have believed; blessed are those who have not seen and yet have believed."

JOHN 20:27-29

Just as the wind is unseen but moves us, refreshes us, and blows over us, the Spirit requires us to put our doubts aside and trust our Father. It's okay that we can feel the Spirit without seeing him. Like the wind, we can know he's there.

WIND IS UNPREDICTABLE

One of the reasons I love the game of golf is because of the challenge presented by the wind. When I'm out on the course and the wind picks up or shifts direction, I may have to compensate by switching to a different club. The wind makes the game unpredictable, which makes it more exciting.

From the cool summer breeze that caresses us on a front porch swing to the furious tornado whipping at speeds over a hundred miles an hour, we know that wind changes speed and direction frequently. Despite the best efforts of our weather satellites and Doppler-radar reporters, we still experience the unpredictability of the wind. It goes where it wants.

The Holy Spirit moves in different ways as well. In fact, there's one instance in Scripture where English translators use the word *wind* instead of *spirit*. Jesus told the Pharisee Nicodemus, "The wind [*pneuma*] blows wherever it pleases. You hear its sound, but you cannot tell where it comes from or where it is going. So it is with everyone born of the Spirit" (John 3:8). Jesus made it explicitly clear that the Holy Spirit moves like the wind, in a seemingly unknowable way.

This unpredictability makes a lot of us uncomfortable. Most people like everything orderly and in its place. Yet the Spirit-Wind can blow through and change that order really quickly.

So if this quality makes us so uncomfortable, then why does it seem to be a key part of the Spirit's essence? I believe it's because if he was predictable, then we'd put our trust in a system—the structure, the kind of cause-and-effect behavior that leads to legalism rather than relationship. Only once did God speak through a burning bush—just once. If we could consistently predict the Spirit's movement, then we would figure out a way to accomplish things without him.

God wants us to depend on him and interact with him on a daily, ongoing basis. Because of our selfishness and inclination toward personal comfort and convenience, we'd rather not have to deal with constant change and uncertainty. We have difficulty reconciling the goodness of God with the mystery of his ways. As Mr. Beaver famously tells a hesitant Lucy about Aslan, the lion representing Christ, in C. S. Lewis's Narnia tales: "'Course he isn't safe. But he's good."[17]

In fact, have you ever wondered why Jesus used different methods or techniques to heal people? On one occasion, some people brought a blind man to Jesus and asked Jesus to touch the man in order to heal him. Instead Christ spit on the man's eyes (see Mark 8:22-26). If I had been the guy who brought my blind friend to be healed, I'd be getting nervous. Spit? Really?

It's almost as if Jesus was saying, "Just so you know the power is not in the method, let me demonstrate this healing in a creative, unexpected way." Obviously, being God, Jesus didn't have to do anything or even say anything; he could have instantly willed it and the man would've been healed (as Mark 10:46-52 tells us he did for the blind beggar Bartimaeus). But by doing something so tangible and concrete, there's a clear sense that Jesus knows our human nature and our desire to pin down a method. He wants our focus to be on him, not on the how.

God's ways are not your ways. His thoughts are not your thoughts. In order to receive all he has for you, you're going to have to get comfortable with the unexpected and unpredictable. You're going to have to rely on him instead of just what your senses, scientific method, or research experts tell you. You're going to have to accept mystery as part of the relationship.

WIND IS POWERFUL

Wind can generate electricity, sail a ship, or destroy an entire city. Wind has power. At the heart of it all, the Holy Spirit, the breath of God, is about power—supernatural power. This kind of divine, unseen, unpredictable power has been part of our faith from the time of Pentecost. In nineteenth-century America, revivalist Charles Finney was a major leader in the Second Great Awakening, reported to have led over a half million people to Christ. While training to be a lawyer, Finney became intellectually curious about Christ but resisted turning his life over to God for a long time. Eventually, though, he felt so drawn to the Spirit he could no longer resist. He later described his first encounter with God's Spirit like this:

In order to receive all God has for you, you must get comfortable with the unexpected and unpredictable.

> *The Holy Spirit descended upon me in a manner that seemed to go through me, body and soul. I could feel the impression like a wave of electricity, going through and through me. Indeed it seemed to come in waves and waves of liquid love; for I could not express it in any other way. It seemed like the very breath of God.*[18]

I think all of us want that kind of power in our lives, even though we may think it's easier to serve God on a merely intellectual level. If we can contain something in our thoughts, understand and analyze it, then we feel like we have at least some control over it. Even Jesus' disciples were preoccupied with knowledge *about* God rather than a direct relationship *with* God:

> "John baptized with water, but in a few days you will be baptized with the Holy Spirit." Then they gathered around him and asked him, "Lord, are you at this time going to restore the kingdom to Israel?" He said to them: "It is not for you to know the times or dates the Father has set by his own authority. But you will receive power when the Holy Spirit comes on you."
> ACTS 1:5-8

Jesus wanted to give his disciples supernatural power; they wanted specific answers about dates and times. Jesus told them that it was not for them to know. In other words, "Don't focus on knowing everything." Instead he emphasized that they should focus on experiencing the Spirit's coming. Most of us don't need more information; we need power. We don't need inspiring words about God; we need the inspired presence of God's Spirit breathing life into us.

An intellectual gospel is always in danger of creating a God who looks like us, one who is our size. People who need answers before they experience God will reduce God down to the size of their own capacity. If we've got to understand God before we can experience him, then God can be no bigger than our own brains. We need more than human effort and ability; we need the breath wind of God to blow. "'Not by might nor by power, but by my Spirit [breath of fresh air]', says the LORD Almighty" (Zechariah 4:6).

The apostle Paul depended on the Holy Spirit. He wrote, "Our gospel came to you not simply with words but also with power, with the Holy Spirit [breath of fresh air] and deep conviction"

(1 Thessalonians 1:5). His prayer for the Christians at Ephesus is my prayer for you: "Be filled with the Spirit [breath of fresh air]" (Ephesians 5:18). My hope is that you will begin getting acquainted with God's Spirit in a new and refreshing way. May you be filled with his life-giving breath and forever changed.

BREATHING LESSON

How would you describe your current relationship with the Holy Spirit? When and where did you first learn about the Holy Spirit? How did this shape your relationship with God, both positively and negatively? I encourage you to sort through your ideas and feelings connected to the Holy Spirit and examine which ones come from God's Word, which ones come from your direct experience with him, and which ones come from hearsay and what others have told you or taught you. My hope is that you will make room in your heart for everything he wants to offer you.

> The Spirit of God, who raised Jesus from the dead,
> lives in you. And just as God raised Christ Jesus from
> the dead, he will give life to your mortal bodies by this
> same Spirit living within you.
>
> ROMANS 8:11, NLT

CHAPTER 13

A FRIEND LIKE NO OTHER

....

[May] the intimate friendship of the Holy Spirit, be with all of you.
2 CORINTHIANS 13:14, THE MESSAGE

I remember the first time I heard about it. I was probably twelve years old, and our church was having a business meeting to discuss it. I really wasn't clear what *it* was, but it was causing a stir. Years later, I discovered that our church was fighting about (uh, I mean discussing) a doctrinal issue concerning the "Holy Ghost." At the time, it was all very confusing because lots of people were saying that we had to stay away from other people who had "received the Holy Ghost." Okay, sounds good to me. I mean, who wants to be around people who are hanging around with ghosts, right?

From that moment on, whenever I heard about people who were gullible enough to believe in the Holy Ghost or who "spoke in tongues," I was wary. I thought they must be in some kind of hypnotic trance. That wasn't our kind of faith; that kind of thing was for the tambourine-and-hair-in-a-bun crowd. Stay away!

As the years went on, I learned to dismantle my misconceptions and inherited prejudices about the Holy Spirit. One of the main reasons was because my own Christian experience ended up being a failure, to say the least. As I shared earlier, I had a belief system but no power or desire to carry out the truths of Scripture. Even after my conversion experience at age fifteen, I came to the conclusion that there had to be more. I think all of us have had that thought from time to time—the sense that there has to be more to our Christian life.

If you're like me, you probably never pursued that thought for long, out of fear of where it might lead. Although I knew there had to be more, I honestly was afraid to go for God's best, to pursue all he had to offer me—particularly when it came to opening myself up to the Holy Spirit. The possibilities seemed incredibly dangerous. In fact, I thought if I really sold out to God, I'd spend the rest of my life as a missionary living in a mud hut in the African bush. I thought I'd be required to go door-to-door and warn people to "turn or burn." And if that's what it would mean to be sold out to God 100 percent, then I was just fine getting by with what I had. It seemed safer to have just enough God to get to heaven, but not so much that he radically altered my life.

> *Sometimes it seems safer to have just enough God to get to heaven, but not so much that he radically alters our lives.*

But my frustrations continued. It was literally like having everything I needed within sight but no way to grab hold of it. I felt like I'd been given the keys to a new car with no gas in the tank. Eventually, a friend of mine invited me to a small group meeting where they began talking about the power of the Holy Spirit. Immediately, my defenses went up and all my fears about that church fight when I was a kid came rushing back. But at the same time, everything in me wanted more, wanted to let go of the old ideas and recycled rumors, and find out for myself what the Spirit was really all about.

So I opened my heart to him. And all I can say is that it changed everything for the better. I went from being a weak, milk-fed Christian to a radical, on-fire believer who couldn't stop reading my Bible and inserting Christ into conversations with my friends. And the best part? I wasn't trying to be a "good Christian"! I was just being myself and allowing the Spirit into my heart, my mind, my life. I surrendered all I'd heard about the Spirit so that I could experience the adventure of God's presence in my life firsthand.

HOLY GHOST STORY

The Bible clearly shows us that the disciple Peter was very close to Jesus. And I guess after being a friend and disciple for three years, Peter should've known Jesus better than most people. Yet when Jesus was arrested and standing trial before the Jewish leaders, Peter was still so weak in his faith that he denied being associated with or even aware of Christ, not once, but three times—right after declaring undying loyalty to his Master. At a time when Jesus needed him the most, Peter had no power to support or encourage him.

Of course, Peter's story doesn't end there. Fifty days after Jesus gave his life and was resurrected from the dead, Peter and over one hundred others encountered the Holy Spirit in a life-changing, breath-giving way that forever altered their lives. Within a matter of weeks, this same Peter, who had been ashamed to tell one slave girl that he knew Jesus, was preaching the message of the gospel in front of thousands. Even when Peter was arrested, he remained totally bold and unashamed of his relationship with Jesus.

What happened on that fiftieth day that hadn't happened during those previous three years? Peter received supernatural power, God's breath, the confident life force of faith, and it made all the difference. How can we have a similar experience, a life-giving encounter with the breath-blast of God?

If you're like a lot of people, especially those raised in church, you may have some misconceptions, maybe even some biases, that make it difficult for you to get close to the person of the Holy Spirit. Most of us understand God the Father. We get that one because we all have an earthly father. We know what a father is like or what a good father should be like.

It's pretty easy to understand Jesus the Son, too. God with us in the flesh, Immanuel, came to earth as a baby in a manger, died as a sinless man on the cross, and returned to life as the radiant Son who made it possible for us to know his Father. Most of us have some understanding of Jesus because we've seen pictures and movies that depict him, even if they're likely not even close to being accurate.

But what's up with this Holy Ghost? If you're like I was for years, it may seem easier to stay away and avoid the topic altogether. We don't have a positive association with "ghosts" and all the spooky, supernatural mystery that surrounds them. That's the stuff of scary movies and Halloween stories, and it's best if those topics aren't brought into our everyday lives. But as I discovered, if we want to experience God's breath of fresh air in our lives, then we must rethink our assumptions about the Holy Spirit.

BREAKING THE BARRIERS

If you spend much time reading Acts, it becomes clear that God didn't give us his Spirit as an option but as a necessity. The Holy Spirit is our lifeline to the Father; he's the One who empowers us to become who we were created to be.

God didn't give us his Spirit as an option but as a necessity.

Notice the response Paul gets from some early Christians when he asks them about the Holy Spirit: "While Apollos was at Corinth, Paul took the road through the interior and arrived at Ephesus. There he found some disciples and asked them, 'Did you receive the Holy Spirit when you believed?' They answered, 'No, we have not even heard that there is a Holy Spirit'" (Acts 19:1-2). Almost like a baby who hasn't yet discovered the voice she can use to speak, these early believers didn't realize what was available to them.

My fear is that a lot of us allow fear, misinformation, and ignorance of the truth to prevent us from relating to our Breath-Giver as well. Many people today have doctrinal beliefs but not biblical beliefs. Some have been told that the Holy Spirit does not operate today like he did as recorded in the Bible. Some believe that the Spirit's presence was a onetime, limited engagement for the early church and that he's either unavailable or unnecessary for believers today. But the Bible never says that.

Some people have been turned off by those who claim to have a Spirit-filled life and are tired of being made to feel inferior, like second-class Christians, if they don't behave "in the Spirit" just like those people. Some people have been turned off by extreme expressions that are not even close to what the Bible describes.

What would it look like if we threw out all our biases? I call it the "fresh-page approach" to the Bible. What if we didn't bring in what religion, history, our past experiences, or other people have told us? What if we had no preconceived notions about the Holy Spirit? What if we were reading the Bible for the first time?

With this fresh approach, I'm convinced we would come to the conclusion that the Holy Spirit permeates the entire Bible. We'd see him in the Old Testament as he moved on the face of the earth during creation. We'd see how he empowered different people, such as David and Samson, for different tasks. We'd see that the prophet Joel prophesied that the Spirit would be poured out on all flesh and to all generations.

In the New Testament, we'd see how John the Baptist explained that the Messiah, Jesus, would baptize us in the Holy Spirit. We'd see how Jesus was anointed with the Holy Spirit and as a result was empowered to heal and deliver those oppressed by the devil (see Acts 10:38). We'd see how the Holy Spirit asked the early church to set

aside Paul and Barnabas so they could embark on their first missionary journey (see Acts 13:1-3). Finally, we'd conclude that the Spirit's
role in the lives of believers is as vitally important today as it was two
thousand years ago.

If we look carefully and comprehensively at the Scriptures, we
see that the Holy Spirit is not a status symbol, not the end-all-be-all
experience, not a scary presence to be avoided. We see that he's simply a friend unlike any other, one who can put the wind back in our
sails. He's not a flimsy, ethereal, floating cloud without substantive
presence in our lives. He's real. He's the ultimate breath of fresh air.

HAVE WE MET?

For the next few minutes, I'd like to introduce you to the Holy Spirit
in a more personal way. I encourage you to grab a piece of paper and
pen or a keyboard so that you can jot down the things that might
surprise you about who the Holy Spirit really is. As we've discussed,
his identity is often mistaken and misunderstood, so it's important
that we grasp who he is and the role he plays in our lives.[19]

The best place to begin, simply enough, is to remember that *the
Holy Spirit is God*. In some instances, Scripture uses the names God
and Spirit interchangeably or indicates their unique Trinitarian relationship. "Then Peter said, 'Ananias, how is it that Satan has so filled
your heart that you have lied to the Holy Spirit? . . . You have not
lied just to human beings but to God'" (Acts 5:3-4). By lying to the
Spirit, Ananias lied to God himself.

Or consider this example: "Go and make disciples of all nations,
baptizing them in the name of the Father and of the Son and of
the Holy Spirit" (Matthew 28:19). So if you ever hear someone say,
"Watch out for that Holy Spirit church over there!" keep in mind
that they're actually saying, "Watch out for that God church over
there!"

Next, we must realize that *the Holy Spirit is an actual person* and not an "it." When we interact with the Holy Spirit, we're relating to a person, not catching a cold bug or the flu. I know it may be bad grammar, but he is a him, and it's so important that we see the Spirit as a person—not human, but still with what we think of as personality. The Bible never refers to the Spirit as "it" but always as "him." If we don't see the Spirit as someone we can relate to and get to know, then it remains tough for us to have an intimate relationship with him. Consider Jesus' words to his disciples about the Spirit of truth: "The world cannot accept *him*, because it neither sees *him* nor knows *him*. But you know *him*, for *he* lives with you and will be in you" (John 14:17, emphasis mine). Don't miss it: the Holy Spirit is a person who wants to relate to us personally.

It's also important to dispel any notions that he's odd or peculiar. *The Holy Spirit is not weird,* though sometimes people are. They may distort things and try to use the Spirit to justify their behaviors. He won't tell women not to wear any makeup. And he won't make them wear too much makeup either. He won't make you line dance down the church aisles or laugh uncontrollably at your pastor's jokes (unless they're really funny). Seriously, I'm tired of people talking about the Spirit the way they do. Satan has lied to us about him and given him a bad rap. We've become afraid and distanced from the One whom God intends to be our lifeline.

Our enemy knows that if we all embrace the Spirit and access his power in our lives, then we'll experience unprecedented revival, healing, and reconciliation. We will become like the church described in Acts where thousands discovered Christ and hundreds were healed in his name, all in one day.

In fact, Jesus said that the Spirit is so powerful that it would be best for the disciples that Jesus leave them so they could receive the Holy Spirit. "But I tell you the truth: It is for your good that I am going away. Unless I go away, the Counselor will not come to you; but if I go, I will send him to you" (John 16:7).

Finally, *the Holy Spirit is our best friend.* If you've ever had a very close friend, you know how comfortable it is to be able to relax and be yourself around him or her. That's what the Holy Spirit wants us to do around him. He's an encourager and a comforter, a protector and an uplifter unlike any other we'll ever have. He knows and wants what is best for us. "The amazing grace of the Master, Jesus Christ, the extravagant love of God, the intimate friendship of the Holy Spirit, be with all of you" (2 Corinthians 13:14, THE MESSAGE). We need to be in relationship with the Father, Son, and Holy Spirit and receive the special gifts that each offers us.

> *The Holy Spirit is an encourager and a comforter, a protector and an uplifter. He knows and wants what is best for us.*

Notice that Paul's beautiful benediction above begins with Jesus. It all starts there. Our relationship with him is unique because Jesus gives us grace so that we may be forgiven of our sins. What Jesus did for us we could never do for ourselves. When we receive Jesus' grace, when we accept the gift that he gave on the cross, then we can begin to experience the extravagant love of the Father.

But many people forget about the daily intimate friendship with the Holy Spirit that is ours once we come to Christ. And yet we need him as our friend every day—to remain connected to God, to talk to him, to feel his presence, and to experience his power.

BENEFITS FROM A FRIEND

Our friendship with the Holy Spirit comes with benefits. To find clarity about the Spirit's role in our lives, I went to John 14–16, a record of one of Jesus' final messages, in which he introduces us to the Spirit and reveals how his presence enriches our lives in every way. Jesus says, "I will ask the Father, and he will give you another Counselor to be with you forever" (John 14:16). The Greek word here for "Counselor" is *parakaleo*, literally "one called alongside to help." Some

Bible commentaries point out that the same word refers to someone who picks up the other end of the log you're carrying. I love this image of the Spirit being a very practical helper and co-laborer in our lives.

Parakaleo can also be translated as "comforter," one who lightens your burdens through encouragement. In his book *The God I Never Knew*, Robert Morris tells about the time his wife purchased an expensive, hand-sewn comforter. She carefully spread it across their bed, then called Morris in to look. Not only was he shocked by its beauty and its price tag, he was perplexed when he went into their bedroom that night and discovered that the new comforter was gone! It turned out his wife had removed it. She told him the comforter was not meant to be used—it was "just for looks."

He goes on to recount the many other items he and his wife have accumulated in their home that look good but never get used: china, guest towels, fancy goblets. This practice reminds Morris of the way we often treat our relationship with the Spirit. He writes, "In the same way, millions of Christians have been given a comforter, but they treat Him as if He's just for looks. If we think that way, we're wrong. The wonderful gift of the Holy Spirit is meant to be so much more than an ornamental feature in our lives."[20]

In fact, one of the most practical benefits of the Holy Spirit is the way he teaches us. "But the Counselor, the Holy Spirit, whom the Father will send in my name, will teach you all things and will remind you of everything I have said to you" (John 14:26). The Holy Spirit is the author of the Bible. He inspired and directed the writing of each book. He knows how to bring each verse into our everyday lives. He will reveal the truths of Scripture to you when you listen. For this reason, I always keep a pad out when I'm reading God's Word so that I can journal or take notes. The Spirit always seems to inspire thoughts, questions, new connections, and applications. He loves to teach us; after all, he is the source of revelation and the power that enables Scripture to begin working in us.

GET THE MESSAGE

The Holy Spirit also helps us share the Good News of Christ with those around us. "When the Counselor comes, whom I will send to you from the Father, the Spirit of truth who goes out from the Father, he will testify about me" (John 15:26). Sharing the gospel message is at the heart of the Spirit's purpose. So many people have tried to make the Spirit's purpose something other than what it is, which is to reveal Jesus to us and help us reveal Jesus to others. What was the first thing that happened on the Day of Pentecost after the Spirit showed up? Three thousand people received Jesus into their lives (see Acts 2).

When he fills us, the Spirit enables us to be more effective in reaching people. The Holy Spirit's job is to give us the words to speak as we witness. We may be timid and afraid to testify about Christ, but we find our voice naturally when we allow the Spirit to inspire us and lead us. "You will receive power when the Holy Spirit comes on you; and you will be my witnesses in Jerusalem, and in all Judea and Samaria, and to the ends of the earth" (Acts 1:8).

Many times I get an impression about someone's life—the struggle or relational challenge he or she is facing—and I feel pulled to share Christ with that person. Recently I watched a server in a restaurant and sensed she was probably having to work several jobs to make ends meet. I left a very large tip and made it a point to tell her that God cared about her. Grateful for my generosity, she told me how she was juggling multiple jobs and how much my tip and prayers meant to her. I left the restaurant knowing the Holy Spirit had been guiding me in that encounter.

The Spirit will also convict us of sin in our lives. He reveals our true condition to us, not in a way that condemns us, but in a way that helps us admit the truth and remain connected to God by confessing and embracing his forgiveness. He gently stirs our consciences and makes us aware of what is true and what will please our Father.

"Unless I go away, the Counselor will not come to you; but if

I go, I will send him to you. When he comes, he will convict the world" (John 16:7-8). The Holy Spirit's role is to put the spotlight on areas of our lives where sin hides in dark corners. You know, those places where we try to justify our selfish choices or deny the real problems. He reminds us of our new nature—Christ's righteousness—and focuses us back to our priorities, our eternal concerns for God's Kingdom. "Whether you turn to the right or to the left, your ears will hear a voice behind you, saying, 'This is the way; walk in it'" (Isaiah 30:21).

Unlike Satan, who is constantly condemning us, the Spirit gently redirects us to something better than the tempting but destructive allure of sin. For several years now, I've had a Twitter account. Most often I send out brief Scripture verses, knowing that God has a lot more wisdom to share than I ever will! A number of months ago, however, a piece of legislation passed that I had real reservations about. As I was thinking about it, a clever but sarcastic response came to my mind. Twitter seemed the perfect vehicle to express my frustration.

Then, just as I prepared to send my tweet, I heard the Holy Spirit speak gently but firmly to my spirit: "I wouldn't do that if I were you." For a moment I wanted to argue: "But everyone would get a good laugh from it." Fortunately, I listened to his prompting and never sent the tweet.

The Spirit not only convicts us, he also will guide us through the many twists and turns of our lives, always reminding us of God's wisdom. "But when he, the Spirit of truth, comes, he will guide you into all truth" (John 16:13). When we want direction in our lives and guidance about certain decisions, when we want to know God's will for our lives, we need to turn to the Holy Spirit. The Holy Spirit will give us an inward voice and witness, showing us the right decisions to make. He will guide us into the right direction in all our decisions. We can follow him and have inward peace.

I was reminded of how true that is just before Church of the Highlands launched in 2001. After much prayer and searching, our launch team had found what appeared to be a great location in which to meet. Then one day as I was driving down the highway, I was sure I heard the Holy Spirit say, "Don't launch there."

I called a member of our team who was surprised but, like me, felt we had to follow the Spirit's prompting. Three days later, we met with the principal of an area high school who enthusiastically showed us around his building and predicted that we would quickly fill the auditorium. The team was convinced this was the place God was leading us.

Once back at my office, I knew I needed to call the manager of the other facility and ask if we could be released from our contract. I needn't have worried. As soon as I told her of our desire to meet elsewhere, she said, "I'm kind of glad. I was afraid you were going to break everything around this place. I'll talk to you later." Boy, was I glad I listened to the Holy Spirit! Launching a church is difficult enough without meeting at a facility where you're not really welcomed.

There's nothing spooky, weird, or fuzzy about the Holy Spirit. He's God, he's in your life, and he's your friend. If you're stuck in the doldrums and don't know how to move forward, then the Spirit is the ultimate wind in your sails. He is God's blast of breath inside you, empowering you and guiding you to your truest self and your most abundant life. If you want fresh air in your life, let him be your friend. It's that simple.

BREATHING LESSON

As we've explored, there are a lot of misconceptions about the Holy Spirit and his role in our lives. If you want to experience a breath of fresh air in your life, then you must be connected to him as your power source. While this may seem daunting or even a little scary based on your past experiences or what you've heard, I encourage you to set aside some time to pursue further who the Holy Spirit is and what his role in our lives should be.

Begin by setting aside your biases so you can start your investigation with a blank page. You might meditate on some passages of Scripture related to who the Spirit is, or read other books that explore this even more.[21] If you ask him, he will lead you to know him at a deeper, more intimate level of friendship.

> You will call on me and come and pray to me, and I will listen to you. You will seek me and find me when you seek me with all your heart.
>
> JEREMIAH 29:12-13

CHAPTER 14

TAKE A DEEP BREATH

··

Follow the river and you will find the sea.

FRENCH PROVERB

Several years ago, some buddies and I went to Florida to celebrate the birthday of our friend and mentor, John Maxwell. He's been like a spiritual father to me, and it's an honor to serve on the board of directors of EQUIP, a ministry he founded to train and resource Christian leaders around the world. I had been looking forward to this time away to relax and celebrate John with other friends and ministry partners but had no idea what a life-changing impact the time would have on me.

One evening after dinner, eight of us decided to watch a movie, *The Bucket List.* I'm not a big film fan, so my expectations weren't very high. But to my surprise, God used the movie as a turning point in my life. *The Bucket List* tells the story of two men from very different backgrounds who meet as patients in a cancer ward. They eventually become friends and together make a list of things they want to do before they "kick the bucket."

If you've seen the movie, you know the wonderful message that hides just beneath the humor: all the thrills in the world can't satisfy the soul like a few eternal intangibles. Things like relationships, laughter, and living in a way that makes a positive difference. Moments of beauty and exhilaration that come from sharing experiences together with people you love. Setting goals and taking risks. Enjoying life *right now, today.*

MY BUCKET LIST

God used the movie to inspire me. At forty-four, I had started coasting through life. I'd realized I was at my "halfway" point and no longer dreamed of exciting adventures in the future. I was maintaining the status quo—a good marriage, five good kids, and a good church. But I left my time in Florida with a goal—to make my own list of things I wanted to do before I kicked the bucket.

Creating my bucket list was more fun than I expected. In my first draft, I quickly jotted down twenty-five items at random, including:

> Celebrate an anniversary in Italy
> Take a pilgrimage to the Holy Land
> Build a world-class ministry college
> Fly in an F-16 jet
> Plant two thousand churches in America and around
>   the world
> Play a round of golf at Augusta National Golf Club
> Write a book (that people actually want to read)
> Go to every Major League Baseball park with one
>   of my four boys

I was amazed how this little exercise stirred in me a driving passion to live a richer life—one full of the breath of God. I realized that complacency in any area of my life would quickly lead to a life void of purpose and meaning, one with no wind, no breath. This is not how

I wanted to live the second half of my life. I wanted more and knew God longed to give me more than what I'd settled for in middle age.

No matter what our ages or current seasons of life, the same thing is true for all of us: if we stop growing and settle into a maintenance-and-survival mode, we'll eventually become stagnant. During my nearly thirty years of ministry, I've seen so many Christians just coasting through life. They've been in church

> *Complacency quickly leads to a life void of purpose and meaning, one with no wind, no breath.*

for a long time, so long that at any given moment of a church service they can predict what will happen next. When the speaker mentions a passage of Scripture, they're already thinking, *Yep, I know that story. I bet he's going to talk about avoiding temptations.* It almost becomes a game for them—you can sense them quietly challenging the pastor or teacher: *You can't surprise me. I know that one. Been there, heard that a dozen times.*

Some Christians have gone through the routine for so long that their faith has become stale and flat, bland and impotent. That's a dangerous place to be. The enemy capitalizes on our complacency to keep us immature, never enjoying God's breath of fresh air. As this book concludes, I want to inspire you to pursue all that God has for you. I want to encourage you to open your heart to a fresh revelation from God, to pursue the Holy Spirit and let him fill your life with fresh air. I want to challenge you to climb to higher heights.

BEYOND YOUR IMAGINATION

How would you complete this sentence: "God is _____"? Most people tend to answer with something they've already discovered about God: "God is my peace, God is my righteousness, God is my healer, God is my protector, God is all-knowing, God is my provider." While these statements are all true, these adjectives and nouns and a thousand more still would not define God—because God is more than we could ever grasp, let alone define.

If you said, "God is faithful," he's still more faithful than you could possibly imagine. If you said, "God is loving," based on your experience of his love, you still haven't come close to comprehending how abundant his love is.

Here's what I've discovered: God is not limited to what we're currently experiencing or how we've known him in the past. How depressing would it be if God were only what you've already discovered and nothing more? He certainly is all that you've discovered—but he's also more than you or I could ever dream or imagine. Scripture tells us that God "is able to do immeasurably more than all we ask or imagine" (Ephesians 3:20).

Could it be that we've settled with our current understanding and experience of God? Could it be that in our relationship with God we've gravitated to an incredibly safe lifestyle? Could it be that we're serving God but attempting to stay in control of our own lives? Could it be that our faith has become so predictable and uninspiring that we're bored and stagnant?

> *If God is the one who can and will do exceedingly and abundantly more than all we could ask, imagine, or think, why not let him?*

Maybe it's time for us to do something drastically different. To take God at his word, even when it feels uncomfortable or vulnerable or unfamiliar. Maybe it's time to let go of the past and pursue his Spirit and breath like never before. If he is the God who can and will do exceedingly and abundantly more than all we could ask, imagine, or think, why not let him? What will it take for us to let God saturate our lives with his love? For him to resuscitate our hearts with his life-giving breath?

OUT OF CONTROL

If there is anything I know about God and the Christian walk, it's that God will always require the big leap from us—a step of faith. When we live by faith, we step toward something and don't know what's up ahead of us. We walk on God's path and can't see what's around the bend. We may not like this uncertainty or lack of control, but the Bible is clear: without faith it's impossible to please God. He rewards those who diligently and earnestly pursue him—all of him (see Hebrews 11:6).

Even when I knew I was genuinely saved and pursuing all God had for me, I remained guarded. I was sure there had to be more to the Christian life but was afraid to go there because of my preconceived notions. The first time I invited the Holy Spirit to fill me, my prayer was a mixed bag of double messages—something like this: "Holy Spirit, I want to receive you, but at the same time I don't want to lose control. I want you to come in on my terms. I'll receive you, but I still have some concerns about you and your ways. If you can behave yourself, then you're welcome to come in and stay awhile."

It sounds like a halfhearted contract with an unruly tenant instead of a commitment of love and spiritual adventure with the God of the universe. I can laugh about it now, mostly because later I became convicted about how lukewarm I was being. Like so many people, I'd let my religious prejudices taint my beliefs and color my perceptions. Finally, though, I said, "I want you and everything you have to offer—all of me for all of you."

If I've learned anything in my relationship with God, it's the importance of not holding back, of going all in.

If I've learned anything in my thirty-four years of relationship with God, it's the importance of not holding back, of going all in. "You will seek me and find me when you seek me with all your heart" (Jeremiah 29:13). It can't be halfway. It can't be someday. It can't be just enough to get by on. It must be total, wholehearted, and beyond your control.

On Easter Sunday 2012, over three thousand people came to Christ at our church's various campuses. In the book of Acts, we see that the first Christians were always baptized immediately after they came to faith, and our team felt that was an important step for these new believers to take as well. So the Sunday after Easter, Highlands held a spontaneous baptism service.

Audrey, whom you met in chapter 2, was there that Sunday with her husband, kids, and her parents. In her blog post, she describes her reaction when I announced this service:

> *This week, Pastor Chris surprised us all by doing an impromptu baptismal service! An opportunity for all those recently saved and anyone else who has not been baptized yet to be baptized today during the service! What?? And he left no room for excuses. They had complete changes of clothes for anyone of any size who wanted to get baptized . . . shorts, T-shirts, and, yes—even undergarments! They even had pony tail holders, blow dryers, and hair mousse for those who needed it.*
>
> *My daughter turned to me with tears in her eyes. . . . I asked, "Are you doing it?" She eagerly nodded yes as tears filled up her eyes and she wrapped her arms around my neck for a good long squeeze as we both cried together. Then I turned to Chris (my hubby who became a Christ follower 4.5 years ago on Christmas Eve) and asked him if he was going to do it and he simply nodded his head and said, "Yeah!" Within the next 60 seconds they were both getting their T-shirt and shorts and got in line with so many others who decided to get baptized today. It was so awesome.*

What I love about this story is the willingness of Audrey's husband and daughter to follow the Spirit's lead, to do something they hadn't planned on. As a result, her family was blessed in a way they will never forget. She ended her post this way:

> *What made today even more special is that my parents happened to be in town to watch my son's baseball tournament*

and visited church with us for the first time this morning. We left church just beaming and filled with joy! What an amazing experience that we will never forget—what a God thing, ya know?

In addition to Audrey's husband and daughter, 1,107 people were baptized at Church of the Highlands that day.

ROLLING DOWN THE RIVER

About an hour northwest of our home in Birmingham is Smith Lake. For a place with such a generic-sounding name, it's one of the most amazing lakes in the country, with over five hundred miles of wooded shoreline around freshwater that's over two hundred feet deep in many spots. It's a wonderful place to play on the water, whether boating, fishing, skiing, or tubing. Smith Lake also features several rocky cliffs along its edges where courageous (or crazy) swimmers like to jump or dive.

The tallest cliff that I'm aware of is over sixty feet, about as high as a four-story building. When I first saw it, I realized that my common sense was stronger than either my ego or my back and that I didn't have anything to prove by jumping. However, as I talked to one of my crazy friends who had to try it, he said, "You can't think about what you're doing—you just have to do it!" Sometimes I think this mind-set is how we should approach our relationship with the Holy Spirit.

In fact, my friend's comment reminds me of another body of water that's mentioned in Scripture by the prophet Ezekiel. He wrote:

As the man went eastward with a measuring line in his hand, he measured off a thousand cubits and then led me through water that was ankle-deep. He measured off another thousand cubits and led me through water that was knee-deep. He measured off another thousand and led me through water that was up to the waist. He measured off another thousand, but now it was a river that I could not cross, because the water had risen and was deep enough to swim in—a river that no one could cross.

EZEKIEL 47:3-5

This river gives us a great illustration of the way in which God calls us to let go of our attempts to control and find the place where he preserves and directs us. In the shallow water, we tend to feel in control since we can touch the bottom. But in the middle, God invites us to swim, to immerse ourselves in all that he has for us.

As Ezekiel discovers, the flowing waters in the middle of the river are life-giving, making the surrounding riverbanks especially fertile and beautiful. Where the river flows everything will live.

Fruit trees of all kinds will grow on both banks of the river. Their leaves will not wither, nor will their fruit fail. Every month they will bear fruit, because the water from the sanctuary flows to them. Their fruit will serve for food and their leaves for healing.

EZEKIEL 47:12

Ezekiel's revelation still holds true for us today. Many of us prefer just to wade in the river, experiencing some of God's mystery while staying in control by keeping our feet firmly on the river bottom. Yet the Spirit of God invites us to go from an ankle-deep faith to one that's knee-deep, then waist-deep, and finally to one in which we can no longer touch the bottom at all—where we are no longer in control of our own lives. One where we dive into the middle and swim in the powerful current of God's extravagant love and abundant joy.

So venture out from the bank. Go out farther, where your feet can't touch the bottom. Experience the exhilaration and adventure that come when you let the river take you wherever it flows.

JUST BREATHE

We began our journey together in this book by looking at the doldrums and thinking about how it feels when we get stuck, and how much better it feels when we experience a fresh breeze, a second wind, a breath of fresh air in our lives. Then we explored how we can reinvigorate our lives by developing habits and practices that make a place for the breath to flow in all areas of our lives. Finally, we moved our focus to the source of God's life-giving presence: the Holy Spirit.

We've come to the edge now, and it's time to jump in.

BREATHING LESSON

Many people are afraid to jump in because they want to stay in control. But the truth is that none of us can ultimately control our lives, nor do we really want to try. We long for the safety of our Father's arms and the intimate friendship of his Spirit. In the same way I put together a bucket list to challenge myself and invigorate my life, I dare you to go for what you long for most. I challenge you to put yourself on a spiritual growth adventure where you experience the breath of God's Spirit.

So what are the next steps? Open your heart to the Holy Spirit. Just like our salvation, the presence of the Holy Spirit in our lives is a free gift. Don't let fear keep you from a real relationship with the One who is breath and who also gives you breath. All you have to do is ask and receive—and get ready for the most exciting adventure of your life.

As you finish reading this final page, I encourage you to

still yourself for a moment and breathe deeply. Inhale and be aware of how the air fills your lungs and sends oxygen to all parts of your body. Exhale and release the breath that's no longer needed. You need air to live. If you don't breathe, you'll die. Spiritually, you need the life-giving air that God wants to breathe into each of us.

Take a deep breath and let him in.

No one's ever seen or heard anything like this,
Never so much as imagined anything quite like it—
What God has arranged for those who love him.

But you've seen and heard it because God by his Spirit has brought it all out into the open before you. The Spirit, not content to flit around on the surface, dives into the depths of God, and brings out what God planned all along.

I CORINTHIANS 2:9-10, THE MESSAGE

ACKNOWLEDGMENTS

To all my friends who offered support, encouragement, and assistance on this project, I'm more grateful than you'll ever know. I'm especially indebted to:

Robert Hodges (my father) and Billy Hornsby (my father-in-law): I learned so much about life and ministry from your godly examples. I miss you both so much.

Roy and Larry Stockstill: Thank you for being my pastors for over thirty-three years. The legacy of Bethany lives on in so many of us.

Craig Groeschel and John Maxwell: You both knew there was a book in me, and I probably wouldn't have written it without your consistent encouragement. Thank you.

Jan Long Harris, Nancy Clausen, Sarah Atkinson, Kim Miller, and the whole team at Tyndale: You exceeded my expectations in every way. Thank you for believing in me.

Dudley Delffs: Thank you for making my sentences make sense. I loved every minute of working with you.

Tom Winters: You believed in this book before I did. Thank you.

Kellen Coldiron: You add so much to my life and ministry. Thank you for partnering with me in communicating the message God gives us.

Karol Hobbs: You're not only an amazing sister but you are also the most dedicated personal assistant I know. Thank you for serving me and this project the way you do.

Caroleen Hodges: You're the best mom ever. Thank you for covering me in love and prayer.

Sarah, Michael, David, Jonathan, and Joseph: Your love and support makes it possible for me to do what I do. You are my best friends and a huge part of this project.

Tammy: You are the love of my life. Thank you for making my life better in every way.

ENDNOTES

1. Audrey Curran is a lifestyle photographer who blogs at http://www
   .audreycurranblog.com.
2. Craig Groeschel, *It: How Churches and Leaders Can Get It and Keep It* (Grand
   Rapids, MI: Zondervan, 2008), 33.
3. Christian A. Schwarz, *Natural Church Development* (St. Charles, IL:
   ChurchSmart Resources, 1996).
4. Greg Garrison and Charles J. Dean, "Reinventing Our Community: In
   Woodlawn, a Blueprint for Rebirth," *The Birmingham News*, October 16, 2011.
5. See http://www.uky.edu/Ag/AnimalSciences/dairy/extension/nut00014.pdf.
6. I am indebted to Rick Warren for first introducing me to these three principles.
7. Barna Group, "Barna Survey Examines Changes in Worldview among Christians
   over the Past 13 Years," March 6, 2009, http://www.barna.org/barna-update
   /article/21-transformation/252-barna-survey-examines-changes-in-worldview
   -among-christians-over-the-past-13-years. In addition to the validity of
   Scripture, respondents determined to hold a biblical worldview also agreed to
   the following: absolute moral truth exists; Satan is a real being or force, not
   merely symbolic; a person cannot earn their way into heaven by trying to be
   good or do good works; Jesus Christ lived a sinless life on earth; and God is the
   all-knowing, all-powerful creator of the world who still rules the universe today.
   In the research, anyone who held all of those beliefs was said to have a biblical
   worldview.
8. Gary Chapman, *The 5 Love Languages* (Chicago: Northfield Publishing, 1992).
9. The comments I made on this verse originated from a message I heard Rick
   Warren give.
10. John Maxwell, *The 17 Indisputable Laws of Teamwork* (Nashville: Thomas
    Nelson, 2001), xiv.
11. Charles Swindoll, *Day by Day with Charles Swindoll* (Nashville: Thomas Nelson,
    2000), 242.
12. Gary Portnoy and Judy Hart Angelo, "Where Everybody Knows Your Name,"
    1982.
13. We are a founding member of the Association of Related Churches, which by
    the end of 2012 will have planted nearly 350 churches.
14. Associated Press, "Consumer Borrowing Soared in November," *New York Times*,
    January 10, 2012.

15. See Richard A. Swenson, *Margin: Restoring Emotional, Physical, Financial, and Time Reserves to Overloaded Lives* (Colorado Springs, CO: NavPress, 2004), 42.

16. If you'd like additional practical ideas on how to incorporate rest into your life, I recommend the book *Leading on Empty* by Wayne Cordeiro (Bloomington, MN: Bethany House, 2009).

17. C. S. Lewis, *The Lion, the Witch and the Wardrobe* (New York: HarperCollins, 1950), 80.

18. C. G. Finney, *The Autobiography of Charles Finney* (Minneapolis: Bethany, 1876, reprinted 1977), 21–22.

19. Robert Morris first introduced me to these concepts.

20. Robert Morris, *The God I Never Knew* (Colorado Springs: WaterBrook Press, 2011), 8.

21. *The God I Never Knew* would be a great place to start.

ABOUT THE AUTHOR

CHRIS HODGES is the senior pastor of Church of the Highlands in Birmingham, Alabama. Under his leadership, Church of the Highlands has grown to become one of the largest churches in the nation, offering multiple services each weekend at a variety of sites. In 2008 the church was named America's fastest growing church by *Outreach* magazine.

Chris has a deep passion for developing leaders and planting life-giving churches. He cofounded the Association of Related Churches (ARC) in 2001, which has planted hundreds of churches all across the United States, and he serves on the board of directors of EQUIP, a nonprofit ministry founded by John Maxwell. Chris and his wife, Tammy, have five children. *Fresh Air* is his first book.

Launching and growing life-giving churches

Are you a church planter or church leader, or do you belong to a church in transition? The Association of Related Churches (ARC) offers support, guidance, and resources in four key ways:

- *We help you start strong.* We show you how to build your launch team, raise funds, form a worship team, develop your children's ministry, and gain momentum—so you can open your doors with excellence. If you start strong, you have a greater chance of growing strong.

- *We reach the unchurched.* With more than 110 million Americans never or rarely attending church, it's critical that we cross cultural walls to reach the lost. ARC is all about helping churches stay culturally relevant—characterized by Bible-based teaching, authentic relationships, and dynamic family ministries.

- *We build relationships.* Solid relationships are the foundation for growth in any aspect of life. As ARC churches multiply across the country, you'll join an ever-expanding group of people who are committed to one another's success.

- *We support financially.* We know that it takes money to do ministry. That's why ARC invests financially into the vision of starting new churches.

For more information, visit ARC online at www.weplantlife.com.

Online Discussion *guide*

TAKE *your* TYNDALE READING
EXPERIENCE *to the* NEXT LEVEL

A FREE discussion guide for this book
is available at bookclubhub.net, perfect
for sparking conversations in your book
group or for digging deeper into the text
on your own.

www.bookclubhub.net

*You'll also find free discussion guides for
other Tyndale books, e-newsletters, e-mail
devotionals, virtual book tours, and more!*

CP0071